GLASS
HANDBOOKS

Lettering on Glass

CHARMIAN MOCATTA

A & C Black • London
University of Washington Press • Seattle

FOR AVW

First published in Great Britain 2001
A & C Black (Publishers) Ltd
37 Soho Square, London W1D 3QZ

ISBN 0-7136-5031-1

Published simultaneously in the USA by
University of Washington Press
P.O. Box 50096
Seattle, WA 98145 – 5096

ISBN 0-295-98154-7

Printed and bound in Malaysia by Times Offset
(M) Sdn. Bhd.

Cover illustration and frontispiece: *Lux mundi*.
Dartington crystal barbeque candleholder: surface engraved by drill, 180mm/7.08in high. The
large letters emulate the movement of a flicker-
ing flame. There are no horizontal strokes on
these capital letters so the 'I', in order to break
the rhythm and to indicate where the words
begin, has been given a contrasting crossbar.
This is engraved by stippling the surface; the
symbol of the cross gives added meaning.

Back cover illustration: *Abstract Year 2000*.
60mm/2.5in. optical glass cube. The angles of
the deeply sandblasted lines are abstracted from
the directions of the strokes which form a classical Roman letter 'M'.

Cover design by Dorothy Moir.
Designed by Alan Hamp.

GLASS
HANDBOOKS

Lettering on Glass

CONTENTS

Tony Gilliam
Ubi caritas et amor Deus ibi est This drill engraved plate is 200mm/7.9in. in diameter.

PREFACE

Many people today are enjoying calligraphy and lettering and others have discovered the fascination and pleasure of engraving glass. The combination of the discipline and freedom of the former with the entrancing and magical qualities of the latter can be dramatic.

This book is intended to encourage not only those who are already enjoying calligraphy but also those who are about to learn so that they will be aware of another medium for letters. It is not a 'how to' book on calligraphy and lettering because there are several excellent books on the subject already available. The methods of working described in the text are intended only as guidelines for those who have not yet begun to engrave; ultimately, each engraver will develop an individual approach. Titles of books on calligraphy and lettering, on glass engraving, and on other relevant reading, together with a list of societies, appear in the Bibliography.

The principles of calligraphy and lettering are simple; they are not difficult to understand and they are also fascinating. Different writing tools make different marks thus imparting different characters to letters. With this knowledge, and by the integration of brain, eye and hand, the possibilities for creating designs on glass are endless. The potential for creative letter design in a variety of styles and shapes is unlimited.

Calligraphers and letterers have a love of words. Combined with this love, the appropriate design of letters is extremely important. If thoughtfully considered for particular words which have been chosen for one piece of work, the letter shapes can enhance the meaning and give greater significance to the words so that the whole becomes greater than the sum of the parts.

Awareness of the part played by space is vital. Whether the letter designs are originated by hand with a writing tool, or typeset, or computer generated, the importance of arranging them all in a given space to ensure a satisfactory overall design cannot be emphasised too strongly. In much commercial 'glass engraving' for presentation there often seems to have been little consideration of either the lettering or the glass object or how, together, they could have been considered a 'whole' – whereas a certain amount of thought, and only a little more time, could have provided a more satisfactory and pleasing arrangement on the simplest piece of glass.

Although calligraphy is often considered the Cinderella of the art world, contemporary engraved lettering on glass is now included in museum collections.

This book is an attempt to record, in the British Isles at the end of the twentieth century and the onset of the twenty-first, some of the work which has been created by calligraphy and lettering artists who have found that glass is a fascinating, stimulating and rewarding medium.

International Proverb; best fruits ripen slowly. Krosno glass fruit bowl, diameter 240mm/9.44in. Deeply sandblasted from below, the letters appear in relief. The design, influenced by the foundational hand, was originated with double pencils widely spaced; if the letter is only a few nib widths high, it is not possible to make the 'O' of 'slowly' any other shape. The words are a contraction of a proverb which is found in many languages. The letters evolve from those shapes seen amongst the leaves of any apple or pear tree. In the collection of the Victoria & Albert Museum.

ACKNOWLEDGEMENTS

I would like to thank friends and members of the Guild of Glass Engravers for so generously providing many of the illustrations in this book, and all the students of calligraphy and of glass engraving who, over the years, have asked me so many questions. My thanks are particularly due to Katharine Coleman for the sequence on engraving letters using the copper wheel technique, and for checking the typescript on historical details and the technical aspects of drill and wheel engraving. Also my thanks to Sally Scott for information on glass for panels and doors, Colin Hayward of B & H Services, Stuart Cameron of Engravers Designs, and to Monotype Typography Ltd.

The photograph of each engraving has been taken by the engraver unless stated otherwise in the caption. All photographs of tools and working methods within the text, and of my own work, have been taken by my husband, David Mocatta, whose constant support is impossible to quantify.

David Peace

The city was pure gold . Panel in memory of Lord Dainton, 900 x 230mm/35.4 x 9.0in. Turner Museum of Glass, Sheffield University. David Peace did more than anyone else in the second half of the twentieth century to alert letterers to the possibilities offered by the medium of glass. Much of his work can be seen in architectural settings on panels and doors but it also includes many private and public presentation pieces.

Peter Dreiser
Wedding Plate

This shallow crystal plate, diameter 405mm/15.9in., with a quotation from Kahlil Gibran, is supported on a small, domed foot. The flowers of the wedding bouquet are deeply wheel engraved on the bottom surface; the pontil mark is hidden by a small single rose. The flowers whirl round a small circle of lettering; the jewel-like quality of the gypsophila is a welcoming element acting as a counterbalance to the heavier flowers and leaves. A renowned wheel engraver, Peter Dreiser comments that he is 'not a calligrapher in the true sense', and rarely engraves lettering as the main subject. A combination, as above, or in abstract designs is as far as he would venture 'to enter the mysterious world of the calligrapher'.

INTRODUCTION

Lettering on glass is not a new concept. Lettering has been engraved on glass for many centuries. The reason was often functional – lettering was used as a label or, as with the so called 'Jacobite' glasses, intended to convey either a literal or a symbolic or a cryptic message.

Historically, engraving is illustrative in character; where a monogram is the main element of the design, this is often embellished with decoration. Engraved letters were based on either handwriting or early type design; some are of weird shape which, whilst displaying a peculiar charm, can hardly be described as beautiful. In execution, some show expert craftsmanship although others do not and, occasionally, the general arrangement reveals a glorious disregard for spacing.

There are very few historical examples where the lettering is the design for the glass. Notable exceptions are the richly decorated glass from the Islamic world and the Dutch calligraphic engravings of the 17th century. These have often been the inspiration and starting point for calligraphers today. Twentieth century glass engravers have produced beautiful work where the sensitive use of lettering is integrated into the design (see opposite). However, there are not many examples where *the lettering is the design* for the glass.

There has been a great resurgence of interest in calligraphy and lettering. This was as a direct result of the initiative, research and teaching of Edward Johnston who, in the 1920s, rediscovered the effect of the broad pen. His students and successive generations of students have maintained the impetus and, today, expressive and exciting work is originated with many different writing tools. There was an almost parallel revival in the world of glass engraving when Laurence Whistler, during the following decade, scratched a poem onto a window pane with a diamond tipped scriber. The West Screen of the new Coventry Cathedral, engraved by John Hutton, further alerted artists, as well as the general public, to this medium. The glass engraver who, in previous centuries, might have engraved with the wheel or the diamond point found, in the 20th century, additional tools – the drill and the sandblast gun.

For the engraver, glass has many fascinating qualities but perhaps the greatest is its transparency. There are many rich and vibrant, but also subtle, colours which are enhanced by this transparency and the great range of glass objects now available offers to the calligrapher and letterer the opportunity to work in the third dimension. Evolving a design in 3D can lead to new channels of thought for the letterer and to a continuing discovery of the intriguing characteristics of glass.

Christopher Ainslie
Bristol Blue Presentation Plate
This plate, approximately 280mm/11in. in
diameter, was free-blown by Rob Marshall
at the Bristol Blue Glass Company in
Bristol. In the 1800s Bristol was famous for
its glass, plain and coloured, and the last
20 years have seen a renaissance of this
timeless art in Bristol. Dartington lead crystal clear cullet is bought in, melted in the
'pot', and cobalt oxide added to give the
rich deep blue colour to the glass.

The design was 'wet' engraved using small
sintered diamonds. The engraved line or
mark does not show up very clearly on
dark coloured glass. To solve this visual
problem Chris Ainslie fills in the engraved
line work with hard setting, coloured, cold
resins and by gilding. The gilded line work
is reminiscent of the 18th century practice
of gilt firing on the Bristol Blue of the period.

CHAPTER ONE

Safety

Safety precautions must always be taken when glass is engraved. Abrading the surface will cause glass dust to be released; working more deeply into the glass will cause dust and, occasionally, particles to fly.

- Sit at a workbench which is at a comfortable height.
- Use a chair which supports the small of the back and allows feet to be flat on the floor.
- Ensure a good light source.
- Wear safety glasses for eye protection if you do not normally use spectacles.
- Wear a face mask to prevent inhalation of glass dust whether you work with water or not.
- Cover any open cuts on the skin.
- Tie back long hair.
- Tie back loose clothing.
- Electrical equipment should be maintained in good condition.
- Electrical equipment should be plugged in via a residual current device. (RCD)
- On/off switches must be within easy, thus quick, reach.

- When changing burs or wheels, disconnect electrical equipment from the power supply.
- Methylated spirit (inflammable) should be stored suitably and used sensibly.
- If engraving is done 'wet', drill hand pieces must be protected from the water.
- When sandblasting, wear a face mask and eye protection.
- When using etching paste, wear chemical resistant glasses, rubber gloves and an overall. Follow the manufacturer's instructions.
- When work is finished after engraving 'dry', the work bench and all surfaces should be wiped down with a handful of damp paper towels which must then be disposed of safely.
- Slurry from the tray used during engraving 'wet' should be disposed of as hazardous waste.
- Dispose of broken glass safely.
- Do not leave spherical paperweights in any position where the sun can reach them.
- Do not engrave when you are tired.

Mankind's greatest invention Four panes of glass 240mm/9.5in. wide and 6mm/.25in. thick are set into a sycamore wood base. The skeletal structures of the letters are broken up and deeply sand-blasted into five of the eight vertical planes. Depending on the position of the viewer and the direction and positioning of the light source, these engraved lines make a jumble of simple marks. The design of the words THE ALPHABET is based on the edged brush; this lettering is surface sandblasted on to the front panel. The skeleton letters form into a conven-tional reading pattern only when viewed from in front. All masks were hand-cut.

CHAPTER TWO

Use of Light

The reason we cannot see clear glass very easily is because light passes through it. If the surface of the glass is abraded, or roughened, the passage of light is prevented from travelling through and is reflected back to the retina of the eye.

The glass engraver creates images on the glass by using the effect of light. When the viewer sees the engraving from the same side as the light source, this is the effect of reflected light; when the viewer sees the engraving from the opposite side to the light source, this is the effect of transmitted light. In a design, the glass engraver can use reflected or transmitted light but can also combine the use of both. The letter carver who works in stone or slate also works with light, but in this case it is reflected. Glass which is opaque (for instance, a panel which has been sandblasted) uses either reflected or transmitted light depending on the side from which it is viewed but, with the correct lighting, this will always have an attractive luminosity.

Light has more difficulty penetrating dark, intense colours. Engraving on the surface of, or more deeply into, any glass made with (or containing) these colours is not so effective for the letterer; although the colours may be rich and exciting, the engraving is not as easily seen. Some letterers overcome this problem by applying extra colour, with special paint developed for use on glass, or by gilding.

Whatever the source of light, whether it is artificial or natural, the engraver will need to evolve the design in the best way to combine light and glass. How the glass will ultimately be used or displayed may not be within the control of the engraver but, whether the glass is clear, or coloured, the most magnificent effect of all is often created by the most natural light source of all – the sun.

Presentation dish. Dartington platter, diameter 350mm/13.75in. An engraved illustration will dictate that lettering should be readable from only one position. The design of the large letters is based on a compressed classical Roman form. The small letters are of the same character but were not easy to engrave in the 'well' of the platter because the drill could not be held comfortably; the engraver's chair had to be raised so that the bur could be used at the correct angle. The detail photograph shows the weight of the letters and their spacing; the N would not be the same shape if it had appeared in the lower half of the design (see bullet point, p. 50).

CHAPTER THREE

Posture & working position

Engraving can take many hours and it is possible to become completely absorbed in the work to the exclusion of everything else.

It is most important to sit at a workbench in a chair where *both* are the correct height for the engraver. The workbench should be sturdy and stable. The chair should support the small of the back; feet should be flat on the floor; legs should never be crossed. A secondhand secretarial chair, which allows slight adjustments in seat height, can be useful when engraving different sized items. If the body is relaxed but supported and well balanced, it will be possible to engrave for long periods without undue strain and, most important, control of the engraving tool will be reliable.

A good light source is essential. Apart from natural light, it is useful to have available on the workbench a table lamp which can be adjusted to any position and moved to provide artificial light from any direction.

During engraving, the glass should rest on a cushion which is covered in a dark coloured cloth. Either the elbows or forearms should rest on the workbench, without risk of slipping off, to provide support for each hand; at times, another cushion might be necessary to support the hand which holds the engraving tool. When sandblasting for long periods, sit in front of the sandblast cabinet on a high chair with back support.

Some engravers use water to help keep down glass dust whilst they engrave which is referred to as working 'wet'. From a container suspended above the workbench, a trickle of water flows down a small tube the end of which is positioned just above the work. The flow is controlled by a small tap (from beer/wine making equipment) fixed to the tube within easy reach of the engraver. The glass is rested on a black rubber mat (a cut up car mat) in a large plastic or metal tray. This tray collects the water and glass dust but needs to be emptied

Audrey Leckie
Firework Fantasia. Blue and clear cased disc, diameter 172mm/6.77in.; drill engraved. Photograph by Robert Leckie.

regularly and the slurry disposed of safely (see p. 13). As water passes over the engraved area it may temporarily obscure the effect of the bur but the water acts as a lubricant, therefore extending the life of the bur, and provides a smooth, silky finish.

Other engravers work 'dry'. With no water to help keep down glass dust, the engraver must wear a protective mask over nose and mouth, and (if spectacles are not normally used) must wear safety glasses. A small brush can be used to brush away the dust which gathers on the glass as work progresses. When engraving is finished all work surfaces must be wiped down and the cloths disposed of safely. Air extraction systems to remove airborne glass dust are used by some professional engravers.

CHAPTER FOUR

Glass

The oldest glass objects were discovered in Mesopotamia and have been dated to about 3000 BC. Over the centuries glass-makers have constantly sought to improve the quality but the basic elements which are used to make glass – sand, soda and lime (silica, sodium oxide and calcium oxide) – have not changed. Today, depending on what it will be used for, there are about 20,000 different ingredients which can be added to these natural, basic materials. The uses for this amazing 'metal' are extensive and the limits continue to be broadened, literally, to outer space.

Glass making techniques, although extensively modernised and commercialised, have not changed for hundreds of years. Combined and heated in a furnace, the ingredients will fuse at a very high temperature and then may be worked whilst in a malleable state. As the work progresses, reheating is necessary from time to time but finally the hot material must be gradually cooled under controlled conditions to prevent internal stresses. Stresses will make the cooled

material unstable and, although these might not be immediately apparent, they could at any time in the future cause the glass to crack or shatter without warning. The engraver needs to be aware that the engraving could also help to cause this.

Glass can be blown, moulded, stretched, twisted, left thick or pulled out to the finest thread. It is this malleable property which has made glass an ideal material for providing a range of items for use in the home and in the worlds of industry and science. It can be carved, enamelled, engraved, painted or slumped (the glass is placed over a 'former' and returned to the furnace for sufficient time to allow the softened glass only to take up the new shape but not to return to its molten state). It is strong (for example, the Glass Bridge in the Science Museum, London); it is delicate. It can be opaque or clear; it can be coloured; different colours can be combined. It can last for thousands of years or be destroyed in a fraction of a second.

Glass-makers experimented and competed continually throughout the centuries to improve the quality of their product. In the 17th century three Dutch makers discovered that adding a high percentage of lead oxide would produce glass of bright, clear quality. One of them taught this to George Ravenscroft in England. Because of this, a growing market for cut and polished crystal tableware and chandeliers developed, but the high percentage of lead oxide also made the glass relatively soft and it was therefore much in demand by those who used the stipple method to engrave.

Glass containing a percentage of lead oxide is referred to as 'crystal'; this word should not be used if there is no lead in the glass. There has been concern over the use of lead oxide in domestic utensils and therefore commercial companies are experimenting with other materials to find a satisfactory alternative. However, any amount of lead oxide which might leach from, for instance, a decanter, is extremely small compared to other harmful substances to which every human being on this planet is now exposed.

The British Standards Crystal Glass (Descriptions) Regulations 1973 state that glass containing 30% lead oxide can be referred to as 'full lead crystal'. Glass containing this proportion of lead has a very high clarity and lovely bright appearance, but is very soft and easily scratched. (It is not necessarily 'easier' to engrave because the bur, although it does not wear so quickly, will go into the surface as though this were butter so, combined with control, an extremely gentle touch is needed.) Glass which contains 24% lead oxide is referred to as 'lead crystal'. The higher the lead oxide content the more expensive an item will be.

Today, the studio glass artist uses tools made from iron and wood which have also changed little over the centuries. In handmade glass, there will be a circular mark on the base of the blown item called a punty. This is where the pontil, an iron rod used to hold and manipulate the glass during the making, was attached. The pontil is eventually snapped off and leaves a scar of roughened glass in a shallow lens. This sharp, roughened glass can be ground away later and the surface re-polished; the pontil mark is usually accepted as part of the character of handmade glass and the engraver will incorporate this into the design. However, if necessary – and if the thickness of the glass allows – this mark can be completely ground and polished away.

It is perhaps appropriate to reflect that mankind is dependent on fire and water to help him to create this wonderful 'metal'. Once the glass-maker has taken a 'gather' of red hot molten glass from the furnace onto the end of the breathing iron, by blowing down the iron he begins to form the red hot molten material into a shape. Due to imagination, technical knowledge, physical strength, energy and skill, the cooling glass becomes the record of a movement – and has an association with calligraphy.

Where to obtain glass

Retail

Large department stores offer a considerable range of glass with tremendous variety in shapes and sizes. There will be a choice between 'full lead crystal', 'lead crystal' and the less expensive 'glass' which may contain some lead oxide. The lead content will always be marked on the packaging of better quality items. (Department store assistants are often unable to give detailed answers to any questions about lead content.) It will not always be easy to assess the hardness of inexpensive glass items until the engraving begins and the effect of the bur is tested.

For the student who is just beginning to engrave it is advisable to choose a simple, straight sided, cylindrical or conical, vessel. Never attempt to engrave glass items intended for use as kitchen or ovenware. (These are made from toughened borosilicate glass which is a sandwich of glass under pressure to give it strength and heat tolerance; if the strong, outer shell is penetrated by engraving, the pressure is released and the glass will explode.)

To acquire a 'feel' for engraving, it is preferable to work on 'seconds' of lead crystal rather than glass. For a first attempt, avoid the inexpensive coloured glass because it is fairly hard; this is because the substances used in manufacture have often been recycled and produce an unattractive clear glass to which colour is added to make it more marketable. However, what is most important is that if one particular item attracts and excites then the engraver should design for and work on this – never mind how hard or soft the material may be!

Trade suppliers

These companies will deal with enquiries from the general public and can be traced through the telephone directory. As well as domestic ware, trade suppliers often provide unusual shapes in crystal and in glassware

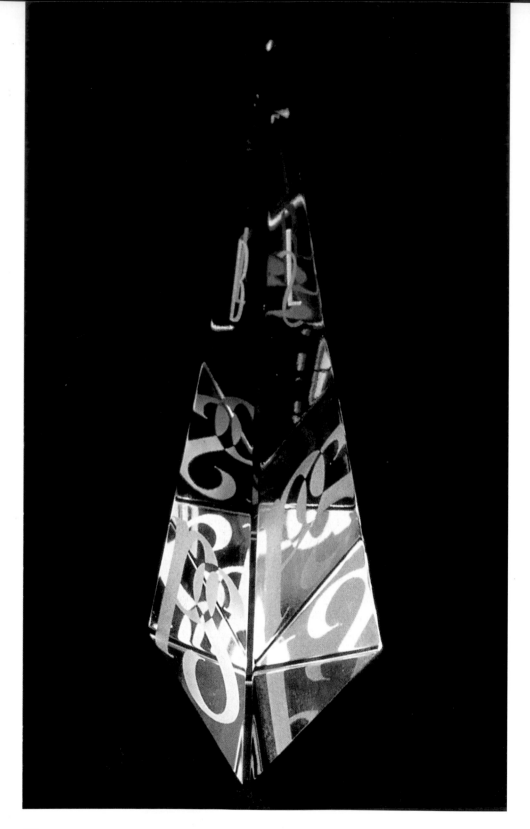

which are not normally seen in retail outlets. Because of their different shapes, these items produce fascinating refractions which can stimulate the imagination of those whose interest is designing with letters. Suppliers are usually prepared to discuss special requirements but this might call for a bulk delivery.

Faults

Before purchasing glass, look at it carefully because manufacturers' quality control can vary from shift to shift. Run fingers lightly round the rim and base to check for any chipping and, against a dark background, look at the surface for scratches – not easy in the bright lights reflecting from all the retail display cabinets. Any air bubbles, or seeds, can be considered part of the making but if they are unsightly, then discard the item. A seed on the surface could become a small crater if the engraving bur passes over it. A seed within the glass, where the bur will not reach it, may be concealed by the engraving but it will attract attention when it catches the light. Depending upon how deeply the seed is positioned, intaglio or relief engraving might remove it completely. Be decisive

PS
A triangular based glass pyramid trophy, 170mm/6.69in high. The initials are drill engraved on one plane only; the three at the top are surface sandblasted on each plane, two in reverse, to read correctly from the front. Intended as a paperweight, the image changes as the viewer moves.

about whether the glass is acceptable or not.

If the glass has been ordered unseen from a trade outlet and then delivered, check it on arrival and report any problems immediately.

The Glass Artist

After the Second World War, the work of designers who had used glass in the early part of the century influenced a new generation of artists. There is now an established Glass Art movement and the material continues to attract individual artists, in many countries, who explore and exploit its innumerable qualities. Objects designed and made in the studio of a glass artist will reflect the individuality of the artist-maker and can be tremendously exciting. There are a number of glass artist-makers willing to accept commissions from the engraver to produce a 'one off'. Occasionally, it is possible to buy glass which the glass artist has for sale.

If commissioning a glass artist, first establish whether that artist works in lead crystal; some use 24% lead crystal, others do not. The engraver should have a clear idea of what price he wishes to pay, the size and shape of glass he wants, and how many, and which, colours. He must prepare all necessary accurate drawings with measurements. The artist-maker will always advise on technical problems and make any relevant suggestions: for instance, aesthetic considerations may require

Peter Furlonger
Tree of Life
Blue cased Bowl, diameter 360mm/14in., made by glass artist Roger Tye. The glass is covered with self-adhesive plastic, the design is cut through this and then sandblasted. In the collection of the Victoria & Albert Museum, London.

certain colours in the glass and this might be difficult if there are chemical incompatibilities with certain colour combinations.

'Casing' and 'overlaying' are techniques where layers of different coloured glass, with or without clear glass, are combined during blowing.

Cullet

During manufacture, molten glass is contained in a 'pot' within a furnace. The 'pot' is made from heat resistant clay but, because it is subjected to such intense heat, it will eventually crack and break. To prevent this, the pot is regularly replaced. With the new pot in place, the old pot is discarded and broken up – including any cooling molten glass inside it. This is usually retrieved and put back into the new pot. However, occasionally, not all the glass is returned for re-use and it is sometimes possible to obtain pieces when they have cooled.

These pieces are called cullet. They will often have formed into fascinating shapes which can be of great interest to the engraver. However, there are hazards associated with cullet. Many edges will be razor sharp; faults and flaws may allow knife-like pieces to flake off and, because this material has not been annealed, there will be stresses within it which could cause it to crack or shatter at any time. It may be possible to ask the glass-maker to anneal it so that it does not shatter on being engraved. Sharp edges can be gently abraded (with a fine grade of silicon carbide paper under running water) to take off the sharpness but this is only to prevent cuts when handling, not to lose the character of the cullet.

Windows, doors and panels

Glass for larger projects will need to conform to Health and Safety Regulations. Before beginning work on any design the engraver will probably need to be in touch with the various authorities, architect, subcontractor, glass supplier, etc. involved, to be sure of the material requirements and of any restrictions or problems. It will depend entirely on the nature of the work whether the engraving will be done either *in situ* or 'off site' for installation later.

Audrey Leckie
Sabina. Presentation piece; cullet, width 130mm/5.11in., drill engraved. The sharpness of the cullet contrasts with the soft forms of this style of letter. Photograph by Robert Leckie.

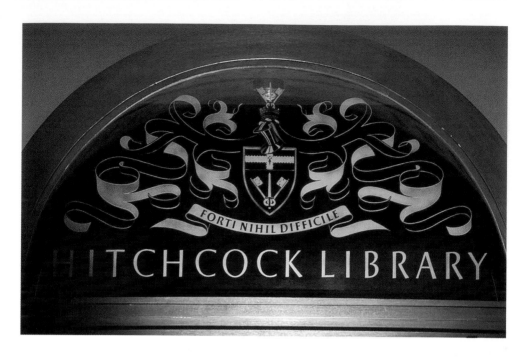

The light source, and direction, must be discussed during the first site visit.

Toughened glass can be engraved but it is preferable from the engraver's point of view if the engraving is carried out prior to the toughening.

Laminated glass can also be engraved. This is another form of safety glass made with two layers of glass with plastic lamination between. It will need to be set within a frame to protect the edges.

Fire-resistant safety glass is designed to resist the heat of a fire for a certain amount of time to allow evacuation of a building. Engraving depth is very limited and, because regulations are occasionally revised, this measurement should be checked with the relevant authorities before starting to design; the fire-resistant qualities will

Hitchcock Library. Panel over double doors in a new library building for a school. The engraved panel sits behind the fire resistant safety glass although the fact that there are two panes of glass is not apparent.

be void if engraving is deeper than is specified. To resolve this problem, a sheet of plate glass may be engraved instead and placed before, or behind, the fire-resistant safety glass.

Optical glass

This is an extremely pure form of glass which is absolutely flawless. It is correspondingly more expensive. Although used in the optical trade in a very soft form, it can also be extremely hard. The great clarity of this glass renders it virtually invisible so that engraved images look as though they are suspended in air.

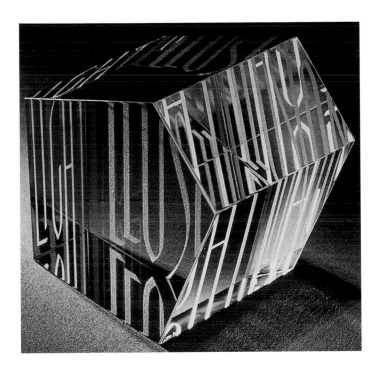

Light illusion. An unusual shape in optical glass, hand cut and polished by John Dawes. The word 'light' is on the far left plane, 'wrong reading ' when seen from the front; the letters were sandblasted through a hand cut mask sufficiently deeply to give them an edge. The word 'illusion', in a different weight and size, is drill engraved on the far right plane 'wrong reading' when seen from in front. The refractions as the object is turned or the viewer moves are intriguing.

Antique Glass

It is not advisable to engrave glass of unknown provenance. It will probably not be possible to assess the quality of the material accurately. Any engraving might cause stresses within the glass which could fracture or shatter it. If it is antique lead crystal, it may be brittle and prone to splintering.

It is important to realise that to attempt to engrave an old glass – of any kind – might be to devalue a unique object.

Ways of using glass

There are three ways to use glass when engraving. The first, when only the surface is scratched or abraded, is referred to as *surface engraving*; the second, when the engraver works more deeply into the glass to produce areas of different, overlapping levels, is *intaglio engraving*; and the third, when the original surface is cut away to leave part of it proud, is *relief engraving.*

JP. 95mm/3.7in. high. The two initials on this whisky tumbler are surface engraved by drill. The flourish is formed from the effect of a broad pen tilted onto a corner as the writing is finished; with first a small and then a larger bur, the end of the flourish is engraved more deeply than the surface (the beginnings of intaglio engraving) and, to provide contrast, is given a slight but not high polish. If written with a broad pen on paper, the end of the flourish could form any number of different shapes which would depend on the speed of movement and how the pen was manipulated; to end a flourish with what is a pure circle is a concesssion to the spherical bur. (The recipient's first name was hyphenated so that the flourish ending has another role.) The importance of positioning the design in the correct place is emphasised when large letters are engraved on a small glass.

In a more recent commercial development, two laser beams can be directed at the glass from different directions; where they meet, they produce minute, shattered areas which create an 'engraved' image within the glass without affecting the surface. Although the innovative glass engraver will no doubt utilise this new procedure, it begins to be removed from the 'hands on' aspect which is part of a craftsman's pleasure.

David Pilkington
Shakespeare Sonnets
Each side of the 200mm/7.87in. cube vase contains a sonnet; surface engraved with a drill. In the collection of the Victoria & Albert Museum, London.

g+d+. Two initials are seen in relief and repeat round this Dartington ice bucket. 160mm/63in. high. They are not engraved; two layers of self-adhesive plastic were stuck together and the letter shapes cut out and placed on the glass.

Small pieces of plastic for the 'ice cubes' were then placed at random, overlapping each other, on the glass. These were then individually deep sandblasted to different levels, leaving the letters untouched.

CHAPTER SEVEN

Methods of engraving

Before buying any equipment or any tools it is advisable to enquire about introductory courses in glass engraving – either at adult education colleges or at residential weekend centres. A two-day course, or preferably a longer one, will give a brief introduction to the craft and the range of techniques to consider as well as providing an opportunity to gather information about tools and equipment.

Since Egyptian times, glass has been engraved with a rotating wheel driven by a lathe; the Venetians of the 16th century worked with the diamond tipped scriber; in the 19th century, acid was used commercially to etch glass. In the 20th century, the flexible-drive drill and the sandblast cabinet provided two more methods.

Two new commercial techniques are water jet cutting and, as already mentioned, laser beam fracturing within the glass.

Wheel

For many centuries, a stone wheel driven by a lathe was used to make patterns on the surface of, and to cut designs into, glass vessels. Examples which can be seen in many museums show that three wheel profiles were used for lettering: the line, to make a thin cut, the mitre, to make a v-shaped cut, and the strap, to make a 'flat' cut with square sides. In their book, *The Techniques of Glass Engraving*, the authors, Jonathan Matcham

Copper wheels: the three profiles used to engrave letters. In the centre is a line wheel; to the left is a mitre wheel, to the right, a strap wheel; these profiles can also be formed on wheels of different diameter and of different thickness.

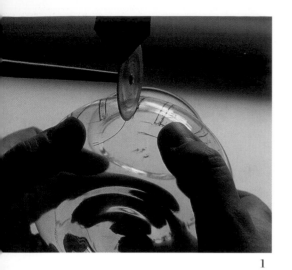

1

4

2

5

3

6

These illustrations show two styles of lettering engraved with the copper wheel. The designs are first worked out on paper then the letters drawn onto the glass with a spirit based felt tip pen.

Each side of the stroke is engraved with a line wheel which provides a 'key' (illustration 1).

With a 'strap' wheel of the requisite width and diameter the main stroke is engraved. Both sides of the stroke may be of equal depth, (illustration 2) or edge cut more deeply on one side, if preferred.

To engrave edge-cut curves, the glass must be tilted so that, with gentle movement, the wheel removes more glass on the inside of the curve, barely touching the outer ede of the curve – as indicated by the impression taken (illustration 3) during the engraving process. Concentrating initially on the inside sharp cut of the bowl of the D, the engraver has to be sure a good shape is maintained on the outer edge.

For a 'copperplate' letter, (illustration 5) a line wheel is used first to engrave the 'backbone' (if drawing the letter with the copperplate nib on paper this line would result if no pressure were put on the nib). The smaller curve of the bowl of the 'B' requires a wheel of smaller diameter (illustration 6).

With the engraved line forming a physical 'key', a mitre wheel (illustration 7) is then used to engrave more width in the appropriate areas to give the letter stroke the characteristic swelling. If the letters were larger, a wheel of larger diameter and width would be used. Six wheels were required to cut the letters in illustrations 5 –8.

The finished glasses (illustration 9).

7

8

9

and Peter Dreiser, comment, 'in the main the quality of early lettering falls behind the standard of other [glass] engraving skills' and that 'lettering, particularly on English glass, is crude enough to set a calligrapher's hair on end'. Today, wheels in a variety of width and diameter made of copper, with different shaped profiles which make correspondingly shaped cuts, are fed with a mixture of oil and paraffin (which lubricates) and grit (which cuts). The grit may be carborundum or aluminium oxide of various mesh sizes. Other wheels made of diamond or of composition stone may be lubricated and cooled with water, or with a fine oil.

However, the wheel profiles restrict the range of lettering styles which can be executed, and the very nature of wheel engraving – the glass is manipulated against the rotating wheel – makes holding the glass, particularly if it is heavy, and moving it into the correct position to 'draw' the letter with the wheel an almost super-human feat.

Considerable time is needed to develop the skill required to produce wheel engraving of a high standard and although there are engravers today who use this method, few use the wheel for lettering.

Diamond tipped scriber

In the early 16th century the Venetians discovered that they could decorate the surface of glass by scratching it with a diamond splinter.

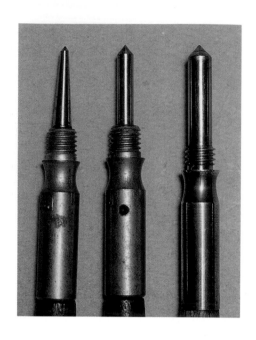

Diamond scribers with points sharpened to 60, 70 and 90 degree angles.

The technique was developed further in the Netherlands in the 17th century and reached a high level of skill there in the 18th; a diamond, set into a holder, was either drawn carefully across the surface to produce a fine line or was tapped gently against it to produce a tiny dot. Images could be created by building up areas of many different tones – from 'black', where the glass was unengraved, to 'white' where the dots, or scratches, were placed very closely together. Compared with the wheel, the diamond tipped scriber was a simple tool to use to draw letters. Examples in museums show that a letter was built up either with tiny dots, or drawn as an outline and the centre left 'black', or sometimes the outlined letter was filled with dots or hatched lines.

Engravers today work with either the diamond tipped scriber or with tungsten carbide set into a holder and sharpened to a fine point. The molecular structure of a diamond will enable points to be sharpened to an angle of 60°, 70°, or 90°. The

Annabel Rathbone
And Caesar shall go forth... (Julius Caesar, II ii). A stemmed and footed crystal bowl made by Anthony Stern, 180mm/7.08in. high. This has been engraved with a diamond tipped scriber.
Photograph by Adam Hart-Davis.

Double ended pin vice; one end has been taken apart to reveal a collet which can be turned to use either aperture; the other fitted with a needle of 0.7mm diameter.

diamond will eventually lose this point and be unsuitable for fine lines but may be used to create rougher marks – for instance, filling in a letter. Pre-sharpened tungsten carbide needles are available in various diameters from 0.7mm–2.2mm/0.027in.–0.09in; the needle is used in a double ended pin vice, available with either two or four different sizes of collet. A tungsten carbide needle will lose its point sooner than a diamond but can be sharpened by the engraver to any preferred angle, whenever necessary. Two methods are: either, place the tungsten carbide needle in the relevant sized collet of the drill, hold a flat diamond coated disc on a firm base; run the drill slowly; keep the tungsten carbide needle at the required angle, but move it along slightly to avoid using only one area of the flat diamond coated disc; follow with a fine grade of silicon carbide paper: or, set the drill in a rigid support with a

diamond wheel in it; run it slowly; hold the needle, also in a rigid support, at the required angle but rotate it slowly.

Acid etch

Hydrofluoric acid is an extremely dangerous substance. In industry, the use of any acids is subject to strict Health and Safety Regulations. Commercially, a wax resist is used to protect areas which are to remain clear; acid is then applied for a certain length of time, before it is drained away into approved receptacles, leaving the glass surface a fine, white matt. For the individual engraver, etching paste may be purchased from specialist suppliers. Accompanying the etching paste are strict instructions for its use. For safety reasons, the acid strength has been much reduced so its versatility is somewhat restricted. Engravers who use acid etch paste or cream usually combine it with other engraving techniques.

Electrically driven drill

Towards the end of the 19th century,

a dentist in America used his dental equipment to engrave glass. In the 20th century, the flexible-drive drill and the hobby drill, both able to be fitted with a variety of shaped dental burs, have made glass engraving accessible to professional artists and to the enthusiastic amateur.

Drills can be divided into three kinds:

Flexible drive or pendant drill

This term relates to the original dental machine but there are now purpose-made, flexible-drive drills available for glass engraving. The motor, working off AC current, is suspended from a support mounted above the bench; this avoids vibration and overheating. Alternatively, the motor can be placed on a cushion on the workbench. This will prevent it rolling, and vibrating noisily on the hard surface, but the cushion must never be allowed to interfere with ventilation of the motor. The flexible cable is laid along the workbench but care must be taken to ensure that the cable remains as straight as possible. The flexible-drive drill handpiece is used with burs of 2.35mm (0.09in.) shank but will take an adaptor to hold a shank of smaller diameter. The speed, from extremely slow to very fast, is controlled by a foot pedal. This drill will run continuously for many hours but the nature of the flexible cable, whether the motor is suspended or resting on the work-bench, makes the detailed engraving of letters awkward.

Hobby drill & variable speed control unit

Available from most DIY stores, this will provide a relatively inexpensive introduction to engraving. The motor is in the handpiece. Different sizes of collet (the holder which grips the bur) enable it to be used with shanks of 1.6mm or 2.35mm (0.06in. or 0.09in) diameter. When engraving glass it is necessary to be able to vary the speed of the drill so a variable speed control unit needs to be purchased at the same time. For engraving letters, it is important to be able to adjust the speed to very slow but, unfortunately, an inexpensive variable speed control unit will not run smoothly at lower speeds.

Micromotor

This kind of drill is smooth running and vibration free but more expensive than the hobby drill. The motor is in the handpiece. A variable speed control unit is required for use with this drill. The burs, of 2.35mm (0.09in.) shank, are inserted and released by a quick twist action. Collets can be purchased in order to use bur shanks of other diameters. The micromotor is particularly suited to detailed letter engraving because it is easily manipulated and runs smoothly at low revs.

Burs

Burs tipped with either industrial diamond grit or composition stone are available in several shapes, sizes, and grades of coarseness. What

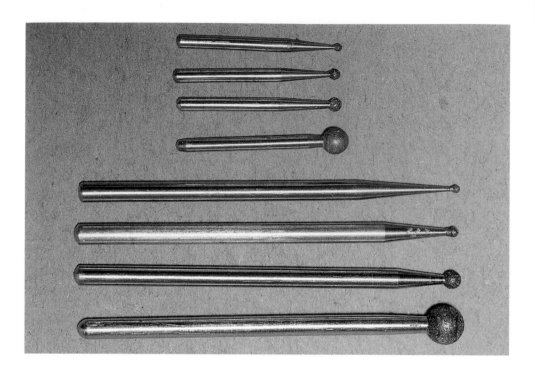

Above Spherical burs of 2.35mm/.09in. and 1.8mm/.07in. shank; several sizes of diamond bur are shown.

Below Other shapes of bur on 2.35mm/.09in. and 1.8mm/.07in. shank; strap, inverted cone and tapered.

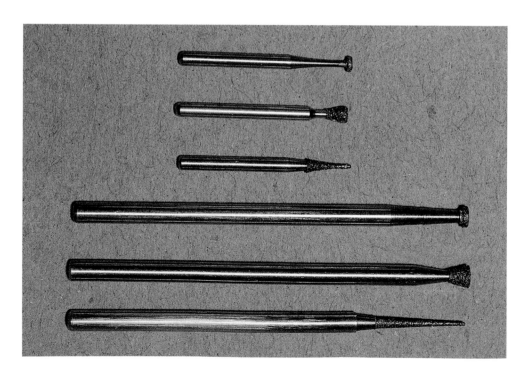

shapes of bur, and whether to use diamond or stone or both, are matters for each individual engraver to decide. *Diamond coated burs:* steel blanks are flash plated with nickel then coated with natural diamond grit of the relevant grade. When the diamonds have lost their sharpness, the bur can be used for smoothing engraved areas but it will no longer cut an unengraved surface.

Sintered diamond burs: natural diamond grit is mixed with a binding material and fused to a steel shaft; as the outer diamonds are worn, new ones are exposed until the shaft is reached. These burs are more expensive but last longer than coated ones. Glass dust builds up amongst the diamond grit during use so, periodically, the bur needs to be run in a dressing block for a few seconds to remove it.

Grades of diamond grit: natural diamond dust is passed through sieves of different mesh sizes to provide the different sizes of diamond grit. (European, American and British systems of grading are not the same.) In Britain, many manufacturers use D grades; D41 for ultra fine; D51 to D64 for fine; D90 to D126 for standard; D151 to D250 for coarse.

Composition stone: burs made from composition stone will give a different finish to the engraving compared to diamond; they are available in different grades of grit from coarse to fine. On a large letter, large burs could be used to cover greater areas quickly. The engraver will eventually decide which kind of bur is preferred.

Shapes of burs

There is considerable variety available for engraving glass but the shape most often used for surface engraved lettering is a sphere. Different diameters can be used depending on the scale of the letter. These spherical burs should be used with a gentle touch so that they do not engrave a trough in the surface of the glass. Some engravers use a tapered bur (often called a rat tail) to mark in the position of the letter, or to draw fine lines, or to 'finish' letters. A miniature strap wheel, or an inverted cone, can be used like a broad pen; these burs will give a 'dished' cut to the letter stroke which is not strictly 'surface' engraving. A large sphere can be used like a copperplate nib, i.e., more pressure will give a wider stroke, and this will also result in a dished cut; the wider the 'stroke' the deeper the cut. There are two sizes of shank on which these burs can be supplied: 2.35mm and 1.8mm (0.09in. and 0.07in.) in diameter.

Sandblast

Wind and sand have always been renowned for their abrasive effect and, together, they can be formidable. The sandblast cabinet is a convenient way to control and utilise this natural method of erosion. Huge cabinets are used in industry, and there are smaller ones which can be used by the craftsman/artist in a workshop situation. A resist (protective covering) is placed over areas of the glass which are to remain clear and, today, not sand but a variety of abrasive compounds in different grades of grit provide a range of textures. Depending on the pressure per square inch, and the length of time exposed to the grit, the glass can be surface engraved, or blasted to different depths.

Masks can be originated by the engraver or stencils can be made from artwork supplied to a specialist company by the engraver. The glass can then be sandblasted either by the engraver or by a sandblast company.

Christopher Ainslie
The Voyage

In May 1997, a full sized replica of John Cabot's ship *The Matthew* set sail from Bristol to Newfoundland, recreating the voyage of 1597. Inspired by this, Chris Ainslie used excerpts from the poem *The Storm* by John Donne and combined these with an illustration, based on a 15th century woodcut, of mer-creatures which might have been seen by sailors in the North Atlantic. At the centre, engraved on the under surface of the foot of the bowl, the original *Matthew* is depicted with John Cabot looking hopefully at an early map of the world.

In this turquoise tinted, open bowl, approximately 270 mm/10.62in. in diameter, the shapes of the ship and the mer-creature were sandblasted first. Chris makes his own 'stencil' from a home produced PVC liquid which is ideal for curved surfaces where proprietary stencils would find great difficulty in adhering without buckling; when dry, two or three coats of the solution provide a resilient, hardwearing stencil skin on the glass which is easy to cut with a scalpel blade. On this design, with the sandblasting completed, engraving was then carried out using diamond coated and sintered diamond burs. Chris prefers to work 'wet' when engraving. An element of additional colour was added to the pale turquoise bowl by filling the engraved lettering with a coloured, hard, cold resin. Chris prepared this using artists' pigments which he ground into alkyd resin. Some of the letters were gilded – gold dust bound in resin – to suggest a 16th century manuscript book. Photograph by Maggie Jenkins

Audrey Leckie

E & M paperweight, diameter 80mm/
3.14in., drill engraved on the base.
Photograph by Robert Leckie.
Audrey Leckie likes to combine calligraphy
with relevant decoration; the decoration to
be an integral part of the whole and to
emphasise or explain the lettering. There is
very little surface engraving in her work, as
such, except for fine lines; the wider parts
of her letters are built up with larger spherical shaped, diamond burs to give a
'reversed cushion' shaped cut. In some of
her work, using small spheres, she will
engrave more deeply into the 'cushion'
shape to make further patterns.

Lida Lopes Cardozo Kindersley

You can't argue over taste Designed by
the engraver, this glass was made by
a firm of scientific glass blowers. They
applied silver at the top and aluminium at
the bowl.

David Pilkington

Sea Fever Crystal bottle with cased blue
base, 200mm/7.87in. high, blown by
Anthony Wassell. The lettering is freely
written all round using a spherical,
diamond bur, with silver leaf decoration in
the title lettering.

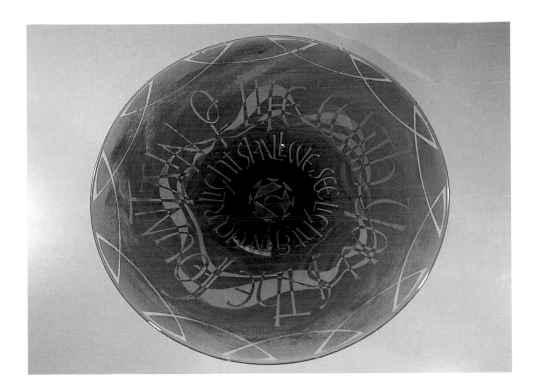

Peter Furlongor

Lindisfarne Bowl

This bowl was designed by the engraver and made by glass artist Neil Wilkin. The diameter is 308mm/12in. with blue-violet cased colour top and a thick layer of blue-grey opaque powder colour on the bottom surface. The design is sandblasted and the lettering appears on both top and bottom surfaces. The words beneath are: *With you is the Fountain of Life* and above, *& in Your Light shall we see Light.*

The bowl was commissioned by the Chaplaincy to the Arts and Recreation in the North East of England. It is a 'candle holder' or 'lighter' – the candles are distributed round the rim or floated in the centre – intended as a focus for a group of calligraphers who annually visit Holy Island, Lindisfarne, to form a workshop in which meditation and lettering are integrated in creative worship.

Right, detail. The letters on the bottom surface of the bowl were deeply sandblasted through the thick layer of blue-grey opaque powder colour. When viewed from above, they can be seen through the transparent blue-violet of the top surface, together with the letters and the centre motif engraved on the top surface. The motif is an abstract version of the Alpha/Omega 'Chrismon', or monogram of Christ.

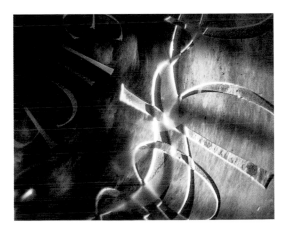

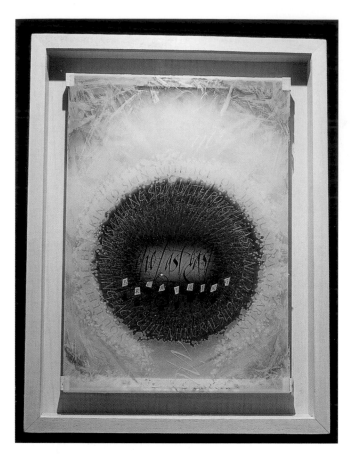

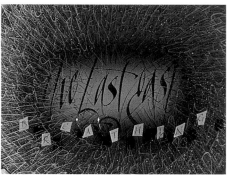

Denis Brown

The Last Gasp, 470 x 350mm/18.5 x 13.77in. Denis Brown works with glass, layered over calligraphic backgrounds on painted papers. He uses multiple layers of 2mm/0.078in. flat glass, each layer 5mm/0.196in. apart (see diagram).

As part of an ongoing collaboration with the poet Catherine Byron, this work is based on her poem *Liadain and Cuirithir.* It is made of seven layers of glass; each is engraved on both sides with writing which overlaps to build the central *texture.* The glass was also cream-etched in places. The lettering was engraved with a tool powered by compressed air which spins a diamond tipped bur at up to 60,000 rpm, that is, 1000 revolutions per second. Thus, speed in writing is imperative. It encourages free, fast strokes but demands great control and discipline.

In her poem, Catherine Byron uses phrases such as 'falling slowly through glass' and 'keeping the cut edges close', in reference to falling in love. No attempt is made to represent the poem legibly but, when viewing the piece of work, it is possible to focus on a particular layer of glass which permits some deciphering.

Above detail

Right This diagram, at an angled view, attempts to illustrate what a photograph cannot; it shows layers of glass and how the engraved texture of overlapping lettering actually recedes, bowl like, through the layers. The small squares, spelling out 'breathing', rise and fall; a respiration in space.

44

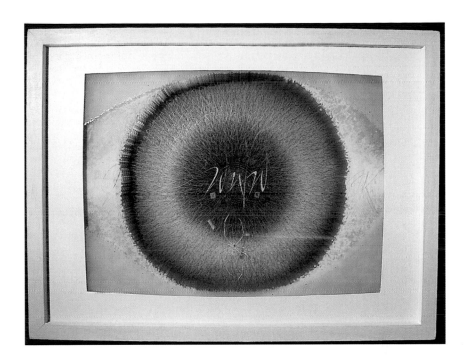

Millennium Bug Trap, 350 x 470mm/ 13.77 x 18.5in.

The spider (waiting to catch any lurking millennium bugs) is not engraved but is formed from blobs of epoxy resin glue and painted with glass paints; the 'dew drops' are made of tiny droplets of the same glue. Denis applies acid etching cream either through a mask or he paints it on free-hand, depending on the effect he wants. The eyeball comprises text from the opening of St John: *In the beginning was the Word...* In this design there are six layers of glass which repeat these words to create a visual mantra – text becomes *texture*. The imagery comprises an 'all-seeing' eye to watch over your computer with a spider's web(site) to trap any millennium bugs

Denis Brown explains that using a small, spherical diamond bur he engraves letters which are directly calligraphic – according to the nature of the tool and the speed of writing – as distinct from an attempt to simulate, through building up, a broad pen form. The letters are therefore basically a monoline but with subtle shifts in quality of line depending on speed and pressure in any part of a stroke, i.e; slower/heavier pressure gives a thicker line; a very fast flick makes the line break up into a dotted

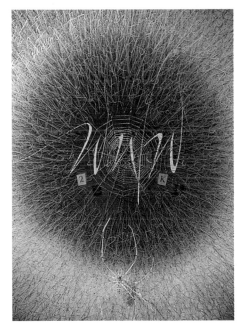

Detail

line. He will sometimes use a strap wheel for large writing to give thicks and thins and these he can enhance by building up directly and freely.

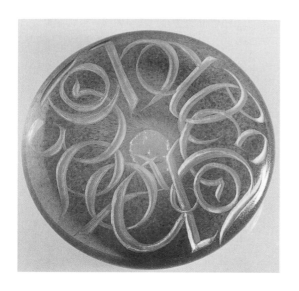

Julian Cole
To have and to hold . For this domed paperweight the design was developed first on paper, then the outlines of the letters marked on the top of the glass with a small spherical bur. Either a small 'strap' wheel, or a cone shaped bur, is used to engrave more deeply. Further work with burs of the relevant diameter finally gives a smooth, finished texture. Julian Cole sometimes polishes her engraved letters with cerium oxide and then diamond paste to produce a high gloss.

Geoff Thwaites
Alpha and Omega Carved 6mm/0.23in. float glass panel 200 x 150mm/7.87 x 5.90in.; the lettering is engraved, and 'omega' is partly polished. The panel is set in a base made of Welsh slate.

Pax Vobis Carved 4 mm (0.15in.) float glass panel with the lettering engraved. The panel is set in a base made of Welsh slate.
Geoff Thwaites uses a cylindrical, coarse diamond coated bur in a drill to carve out the open areas. The edges are smoothed with finer diamond and stone burs and, finally, by hand with emery paper. The lettering is engraved and sometimes partly polished with grit-impregnated rubber wheels

Lida Lopes Cardozo Kindersley

Birthday Present The engraver comments that the bowl was 'asking for lettering'. She designed a sans serif 'or, more precisely, an embrio serif, meaning it is to all intents and purposes a serifed letter except that it has no serifs!'.

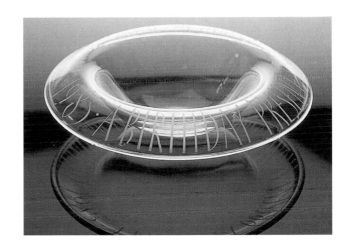

Hilary Virgo *Sheep Count.* A large, shallow dish, drill engraved; diameter 360mm/14.17in. The fleeces have been slightly 'polished' in certain areas.

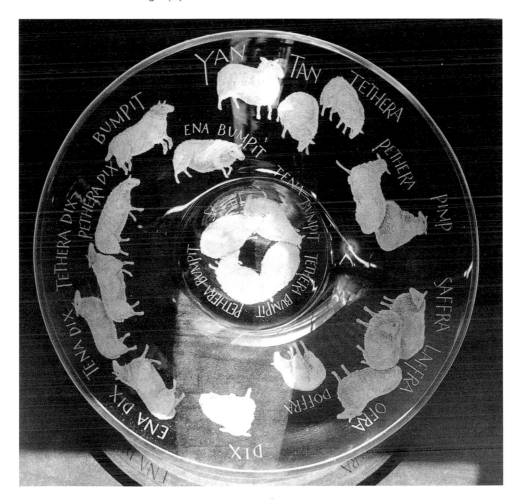

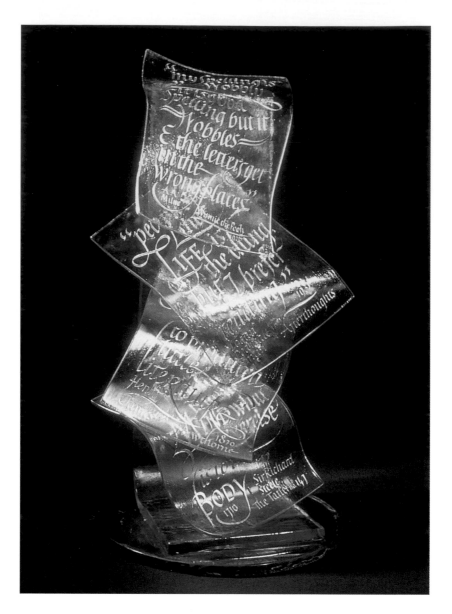

Christopher Ainslie

Lettered Glass Structure.

This is one of two which were approximately 1000mm/39.3in. high and were
produced in conjunction with the glass
sculpture artist, Colin Reid, for the
entrance to the library on a Scandinavian
cruise liner. Before any lettering or construction work could take place five pieces
of plate glass measuring 420 x 297mm/
16.5 x 11.7in. had to be slumped into
flowing forms. The glass was slumped by
Colin Reid. The lettering was designed and
the artwork produced by the engraver.
From the artwork, large, electronically cut
stencils were made. These were applied to
the slumped plate glass which was then
very deeply sandblasted. This stage of the
process was carried out by a London firm
who specialise in this work as also was the
gilding (using a technique secret to the
firm in question) which resulted in a highly
burnished, mirror-bright finish to each
letter. The five completed glass panels
were then assembled into the structure
illustrated.

CHAPTER EIGHT

Inspiration & implementation

Already, the piece of selected glass has an individual, inherent beauty. The engraver must handle and turn the piece and begin to visualise how it can be used. The comment, 'the irregularity of direct inspiration', is very true; an idea can arrive in a flash – to be developed further – or it may take weeks or years to gestate. Sometimes a piece of glass can immediately inspire an idea for a word or quotation or, conversely, it will be a word or a quotation which demands a search – perhaps a long one – for the appropriate piece of glass. Every piece of glass has its own positive character and, because of this, occasionally an idea will not 'work' despite much effort to make it. In this case, perhaps the engraver is not working *with* the glass?

The shape and function of every glass item will influence the decision about the style of lettering, whereon the glass it will best be placed, and therefore how an idea might be developed. Presentation pieces will often be for display only whilst others may be intended for constant use. The goal is to produce well designed letters, appropriate to the glass, with well executed engraving. The first thing which will strike the observer will be the design; if on closer inspection, the workmanship is superb then this will be a bonus and will give greater value to the whole. Good technique is important; there is often reference to the delight of seeing the mark of the tool but this only applies if the tool has been used skilfully. It may seem a simple project to create the written word on glass and the engraver should endeavour to make it seem as though this has been achieved spontaneously and effortlessly.

First questions
• Will the item be seen from below; for example, a panel over a door? Or at eye level when standing, or when seated? Or from above; for example, glass let into the floor?

- When looking down into a circular object such as a wide bowl or a disc, should the letters read from 'inside' the circle (tops towards the circumference) or from 'outside' (tops towards the centre)? The particular letters needed often dictate how a design should be resolved. Consider whether the letters or the *spaces between* them should be 'wedge shaped' – whatever the decision, extremely subtle adjustments will be needed to the shape of most letters, particularly those with parallel sides such as capitals 'H' and 'N' and those which are particularly wide such as 'M' and 'W', and 'm' and 'w'.

- If the words are to form a completed circle, whether horizontally placed on a shallow dish or vertically on a goblet or decanter, how should the first letter in the quotation be defined? Does it need to be?
- Where should a design be placed on a jug or tankard if it is to be held in the right hand?

Every letter is a combination of marks and spaces but usually it is only the marks which are 'seen'. Space is a vital and extremely subtle part of calligraphy and lettering. The student is aware that there are spaces within letters, outside letters, between letters, between words (often

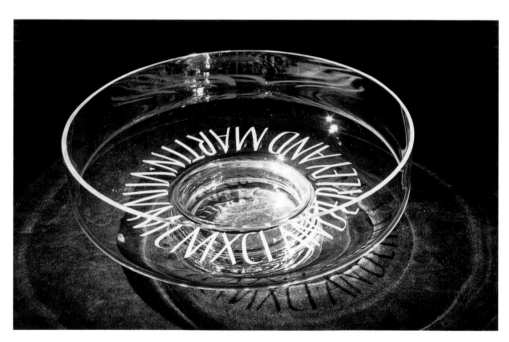

Anderley and Martin. Krosno fruit bowl, diameter 240mm/9.44in. These are deliberately stark capital letters but the shape of the glass as the bowl joins the stem has caused a slight curve at the tops to soften the effect. The words needed soon indicat-

ed that the letters should be placed with the tops to the centre. The spaces between are wedge-shaped. The letters are deeply sandblasted from below because this bowl is intended for daily use and cleaning should be made easy.

too much), between lines and, finally, surrounding the whole. In music, rhythm is expressed by the timing of beats, and in writing, rhythm is expressed by the spaces. From the natural movement of the scribe's hand as the letters are written and from the pace at which the hand moves, so the letter shapes form, the spaces appear and the writing pattern evolves – this applies as much to a line of capitals as it does to minuscule, or lower case, letters.

Both handwriting and typography share this maxim: the reader's eye should be able to travel comfortably along a line of writing without conscious effort. In book design, the typographer should not come between the author and the reader. If the line is too long for the size of letter, then reading it will become an effort; the eye should then be able,

Hadeland Bowl. Scandinavian handmade crystal bowl, not quite circular, diameter 350mm/13.77in at its widest part. A form of uncial, in two weights, was used here, and although this does not lend itself to flourishes, an appropriately simple one indicates where the eye should begin to read.

also without effort, to find where the following line begins but if this line is too close to the first there will be further visual aggravation. So a calligrapher's problem when organising a quotation will also apply to the glass engraver when arranging a quotation on glass. If the whole surface area of a bowl, goblet or decanter is to be used then the problem can become complex.

If the design of the letter is somewhat removed from the conventional symbol for it, the reader should nevertheless be able to decipher the letters – the words should be *readable.*

Shards This is an exercise in letter making from isosceles triangles which are reminiscent of the shards formed by broken glass. In attempting to develop an alphabet in an unusual form, some letters will work better than others. To make this design

more complex, two panes of glass were used, and bear different parts of the letters on three of the four planes. The first illustration shows one pane turned round – 'flipped' – and out of sequence; the second – the interaction of shapes and spaces.

More specific questions

It may be helpful to ask the questions: *what? why? how?* and *when?* Sometimes the last two will influence the first two. When working to commission, the client's wishes should be carefully considered. Other considerations are:

- What are the words? How much can they be altered?
- What is the glass for? What shape is it to be?
- Who will be the recipient – is it someone who will respond to 'traditional' or to innovative design?
- What is the significance of the words and what style of letter will be the most suitable?
- What sort of texture (visual not physical) will be best for the shape of the glass and for the words?

- Should the letters be upright or with a slight lean, and with what weight – the width of stroke compared with the height?
- Should the letters be capital or minuscule?
- If there are ascenders and descenders how may they influence the design, i.e. if there are more ascenders than descenders should the letters be positioned low down on the glass to give more space above for flourishes, or vice versa?
- Will flourishes be appropriate?
- On a long quotation, how many lines should the words make?
- How many different arrangements can be made of these lines?
- At which word should a new line begin?
- How much space should there be between the lines?

- How much space outside all the lettering, i.e., how well does the arrangement fit with the glass?
- If dates are needed, how might the numbers be treated? They can be written in words, or in numerals. The numerals can be the same height as the lowercase letters or as the capitals; they can have ascenders and descenders. Abbreviations can be arranged in several ways, e.g. 1 March 2000 or 1 3 2000 or 1 03 2000 or 1 III 2000 and many more; the *st*, *nd*, *rd*, and *th* should be either a bold part of the design or, prefer-ably, omitted. Note that in different countries, month and day may be expressed in an alternative sequence.
- Punctuation has been developed over the centuries to help the reader; punctuation marks divide areas of text so that the sense of the words is quickly understood. Only when repeating a quotation should the original punctuation marks be reproduced accurately (this can be done discreetly so that

What wond'rous life... ! Krosno deep fruit bowl, diameter 220mm/8.66in., drill engraved. The quotation is part of a verse from Andrew Marvell's poem *The Garden*. The word are arranged so that the lines may be read comfortably as the bowl is turned slowly without having to move it back and forth.

Bicycle decanter. Dartington crystal wedding present, drill engraved. The recipients were keen cyclists, so the engraving on the stopper is not a cryptic message but there is subtlety in the design of the lettering which could resemble a wheel, but, more importantly, continuity, so there is no obvious place where reading should begin.

the marks do not draw unnecessary attention); at other times, the engraver should decide what punctuation, if any, is needed.

- For a presentation piece it is not always necessary to keep to the usual 'presented to X on the occasion of Y' and a few questions to the client and a tactfully suggested alternative way to convey the same message could result in a more interesting solution.
- Enquire if any cryptic symbols or messages can be incorporated which will have significance only for the recipient.

Originating the letters
Pen made letters
In a beautiful piece of calligraphy there is a subtle combination of discipline and freedom revealed in the consistent but not rigid rhythm of repeated shapes which flow comfortably from the hand; the confidence of the scribe and the enjoyment in writing is evident and the letters are full of life. Letters which are recreated on glass must also exude this enjoyment and vitality.

There are no short cuts to becoming 'good at' calligraphy and lettering; improvement will come gradually with continual practice and by using a variety of writing tools. Appreciation of the proportions of the classic Roman letter and the understanding that different writing tools can be employed to make different shapes, will provide a foundation for infinite experiment

with letter design. Working with any writing tool with the intention of transposing the images created by it onto glass will increase appreciation of the subtlety of the twenty-six symbols of the Western alphabet.

The design of the letters of the Western alphabet with their thick and thin strokes is a result of the marks made by the quill. There is a great pleasure in seeing a page of calligraphy written with a tool which makes these 'opposite' marks. An experienced scribe, using either quill, broad pen, reed pen or copperplate nib, can produce beautifully consistent and exciting calligraphy. We now accept that the development of the classic Roman letter was influenced by the 'edged brush'; this was used to lay out inscriptions prior to the letters being made permanent by cutting with the chisel. This brush looks like a broad pen but there the comparison ends; it is kept at a right angle to the writing surface and only the tips of the bristles are used (Eastern calligraphy not only uses a different shaped brush but the brush is manipulated differently). Calligraphers who have mastered the 'edged brush' as a writing tool are able to produce some of the most subtle and elegant shapes to be seen.

The word calligraphy means 'beautiful writing', derived from the Greek word *kallos*, beautiful, and *graphien*, to write. Writing tools were originally developed for writing on specific surfaces – the reed on papyrus, the quill on vellum and the

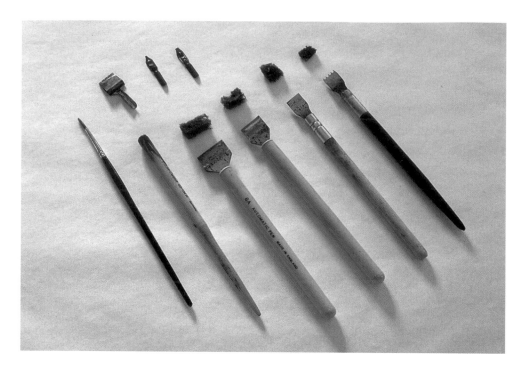

Above Different widths of larger sizes of broad pen; to help control the flow of the writing medium, small pieces of synthetic sponge can be inserted inside the metal. The brush is used to load the pen with, in this case, black gouache paint.

Below Double writing tools adjusted to form strokes of various widths. It is preferable for balance to keep both pencils a similar length, and also of the same grade of lead. For hand engraving, these will produce a precise image to transfer to the glass.

metal pen on paper – but calligraphers today will use quill on paper and metal pen on vellum and they will often make their own writing tools from wood, wood veneer, bamboo, plastic with sponge, or any other material which can be adapted to hold, and then deliver, a writing medium. There are, however, not many calligraphers and/or engravers who 'write on glass'.

In writing, the sense of touch plays a vital role. The quill is the most sympathetic writing tool; if correctly cured, it is firm yet pliable (it may be pressed to give a wider mark but will spring back to the width to which it was originally cut); the reed is a rather stiff tool (a comparable stiffness is found in the broad felt tip pen); the flexibility of the broad metal nib, used in a pen holder, can vary slightly depending on the metal. These tools need no pressure to form the thick and thin marks. Conversely, the thick and thin marks of the copperplate nib are made by deliberately varying the pressure in order to splay the tip of the nib and here the third dimension becomes important. The character of a hand can be greatly changed by subtle alterations to pen angle, letter shape, weight and angle of lean: so, pages with identical text can be written to look quite different.

The image to be engraved should be originated to the desired scale with the appropriate size of writing tool. The broad edged nib is available in large versions for display purposes, and chisel edged brushes are also made in different sizes. Although the image made by any writing tool can be enlarged or reduced by using the photocopying machine, this process can often cause distortion. Any alterations to scale should be minimal. If it is possible to use a writing tool which will provide an outline of the letter stroke, this is a simple and particularly useful way to work because of the method of transferring the drawing to the glass (see p.70).

Drawn letters

The capital 'I' and capital 'O' are referred to as the mother and father of the alphabet. Once the character of these two letters has been established in relation to each other, the design for the other twenty four, and the nine numerals and zero, can be developed. The shape of the capital 'I' will provide the shape of all the main stroke of letters which have a vertical and/or a diagonal; the capital 'O' will provide the shape for the letters which use part of this letter in their construction. The letters can be designed with serifs or without (sans serif). An alphabet of lowercase letters can be designed with the same characteristics.

Devising an alphabet is a challenge but the more time spent working with letter shapes, the more is learned about their simplicity – and their complexity.

Typeset letters

Originating designs on glass from type may be rightly considered as

Tom Perkins
The kindly fruits of the earth. 200 mm/
7.87in. diameter. This is one of the few
pieces of glass engraved by letter carver
Tom Perkins. He is widely known for his letter design and works usually in stone or
slate. Photograph by John Edward Leigh.

somewhat removed from creativity
but can be justified on some occa-
sions. If the letters required are to be
very small (there is very little
pleasure engraving letters less than
10mm/0.4in. high), or if the text
required for a commission is exten-

sive and the fee will not cover the
amount of work which calligraphy
demands, or if the design is required
urgently, then to provide camera-
ready artwork for a commercially
made stencil and to use this to sandblast the lettering might be the
answer.

Specialist trade typesetters who
work with beautiful display fonts cast
in metal are now, sadly, very difficult
to find so most printers, as do many
individuals, originate type on the
computer.

Computer generated letters

The time span from when the first letters, modelled on the thick and thin marks made by the quill, were cut into wood and printed as one page (appearing as white letters on black), to movable wooden type, to metal type, to phototypesetting, was approximately 400 years but in the last quarter of the 20th century technological development accelerated at an amazing pace. The computer revolutionised all stages of printing.

Alfred Fairbank, in his *A Book of Scripts*, comments, 'The significance of the relationship between scripts and printing types is that printing has preserved Renaissance letter forms and has set a high standard of legibility... .' To design a typeface requires considerable knowledge and skill but the advent of the computer has enabled anyone to try and, as a result, there are a great number of styles available at the touch of a button. Many of these are 'uncomfortable' to read. The Monotype Corporation was founded at the end of the 19th century in Britain to exploit an American invention to mechanise the composition and casting of texts in printing plants. It was commercially wise to develop and manufacture at the same time the matrices for the different typefaces needed by the printers and publishers who bought the machines. The rigorous standards of accuracy employed at the engineering works were also applied in the Type Drawing Office; this earned the company a reputation for high standards in type design as well as in manufacture. In 1992 the Monotype Corporation was re-established as Monotype Typography Ltd. Their CD ROM disks provide fonts designed by experienced letterers and type designers and these are available for the general market. The 'Monotype CD ROM' range is being developed continually.

Care should be taken when making an aesthetic decision about which font to use and, with a commission for a company, it might be possible to select one which relates to, or is the same as, the 'house style'. A computer-generated design should be given as much consideration as any other; the decision about what style, weight and size of letter and the overall layout should be worked out carefully with the function in mind.

The meticulous craft of typesetting by the compositor is no longer practised but the calligrapher, aware of the values of word and line spaces, can improve the appearance of text printed by a computer. In a line, or a passage, of capital letters, word spaces and every letter space can be adjusted; the space produced by combinations of capitals 'L' followed by 'A', and 'C' followed by 'T', can be counteracted by individually letter spacing the other letters. For an area of lowercase text, it might also be an advantage to alter the line space using the default setting, or to alter it line by line. Increasing the print quality, from 360 to 720 dpi or more, and printing onto a coated paper will help to provide good resolution for any image which is to be made into a stencil. (See p. 81 for the different kinds of stencil.)

Computers do not always 'speak' to each other. If the design has been organised with care on one computer and put on disk, another might not reproduce the information as accurately. Time and effort will have been lost and, worse, the work will not look as carefully designed as it should. Regrettably, the final result might be referred to as 'a wasted opportunity'.

Developing a design for a goblet

For a first attempt at drill engraving, a 'second' of good quality lead crystal of simple shape such as a cylindrical beaker or a conical goblet is recommended. The lettering should be surface engraved only. Do not yet work on a glass which has multiradial curves – where the surface curves in more than one direction – because these present practical (as well as aesthetic) problems. The design of the lettering can be as adventurous, or as cautious, as confidence permits but a simple letterform is preferable. Do not choose a quotation – not even a short one. One short word or the initials of a friend will be quite sufficient – think of the design as a simply organised group of shapes.

Until the engraver is very experienced, it is not recommended that letters are drawn with a marker pen directly onto the glass with the intention of building up all the strokes to the required width during the engraving. Nor is it recommended that the glass is covered in white paint and the letters drawn into this with a marker pen, or their shape scraped out of the paint with a cocktail stick. When engraving begins, the bur will make a white mark on the surface of the glass which will be indistinguishable from the paint, and the paint will clog the bur. Also there will be many confusing lines on the glass and thus plenty of room for error; any adjustments to letterform, or to spacing, attempted whilst engraving can produce problems which will not only make the engraving take longer but will also take away much of the pleasure.

Every engraver will wish to develop a personal method of working. The following information is therefore provided only as a suggestion – although this system has proved itself for many years.

Make sure the workbench is free of dust and grit; remove metal equipment and work with only wood or plastic; keep scissors at a safe distance. Keep the glass close by for physical and visual reference.
- Decide where the design will be – all the way round or in one area.
- A wine glass intended for use at table will be viewed from slightly above, and the glass will be turned – not the viewer. (A wine glass for presentation only will probably be static and viewed from shoulder

From several trials on the glass, one will provide an idea which can be developed using writing tool on paper. Some engravers work on the glass with coloured felt tip pens but white wax crayon or white gouache paint will provide a more realistic effect.

level or from other, perhaps limited, positions.)

- If the design is to be a monogram, letters will 'disappear' at each side so decide on the width where the design will be 'comfortably' seen.
- Avoid the 'visual interference' at the join of the bowl to the stem when looking at the glass from slightly above.
- On mass-produced items, do not engrave closer than 12mm/0.47in. to the rim. (During manufacture, the rim is temporarily reheated in order to trim it and the subsequent cooling can result in a fault, or stress line, all round the rim at about this level. If any engraving is carried into and above this stress line it can cause the glass to break along the stress line *at any time*. This will not apply to handmade items.)

Try a few ideas on the glass, first, using either white paint or a white wax pencil. Notice what happens to the 'design' when it is viewed from different levels and as the glass is turned. This will help to sort out how the idea can be developed and what is best avoided.

Measuring the area available
Two suggestions are given which can be easily applied to simple shapes. ONE: wrap layout paper all round the glass, trim off excess above and below. Draw horizontal lines to indicate the highest and lowest part of the area which can be engraved.

To mark a horizontal line: illus. 1 & 2. Select a stable support of the correct height; hold the marker pen firmly on this and rotate the glass against the pen.

1

2

To mark a vertical line: illus. 3. Position the glass before a square-sided box; hold a marker pen horizontally onto the side of the box so that, *if the pen were extended through the glass it would become its diameter.* Using the side of the box as a guide and support for the hand, run the marker pen up, or down, the glass. Twist the glass round for the next line. (This method can be used on many different shapes of glass by extending or withdrawing the marker pen whilst continuing to use the box as a guide and support.)

3

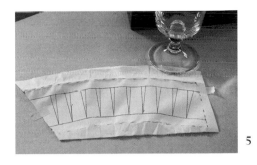

5

To mark an angle for italic: illus. 4. Place a small object, for example, an eraser, or a pencil, or a thin book, beneath one side of the box to tilt it so that the pen marks the required angle. Repeat the method as for vertical lines. To increase or decrease the angle, place a thicker or thinner item beneath the side of the box. Unwrap and lie the paper flat as a template. Working within this area, determine the size and style of the letters; draw extra lines on to the template as required. Place the template beneath each new sheet of layout paper as the design is developed. It should be possible to secure the final drawing to the glass with only minor adjustments to the fit by extending or reducing the space at the join.

Two: (illustration 6) wrap a narrow strip of layout paper round the glass to determine length of line; note depth of working area and decide on height of letter. Measure the length of line; mark this on a drawing pad of layout paper and design the letters within this area. Unless the glass is truly cylindrical, it will be necessary to 'release' the paper with the final design before securing it to the glass; snip from above *and* below the letters, and slightly *between* each (not between the strokes of any one letter which could distort its shape). The drawing can be secured to the glass with minor alterations to the space at the join.

With further experience, the engraver will know which method will be preferable and also how to deal with a more complicated shape.

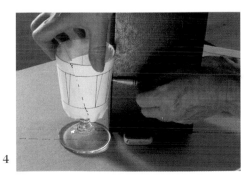

4

6

Marking the glass

This can be done the same way as shown in *Measuring the area available* but keep the lines drawn on to the glass to a minimum. Too many can become confusing. Marks from water-based felt tipped marker pens are quickly removed with water and paper tissue (or cotton wool) and from spirit-based pens with methylated spirit. Keep all guide lines, drawn with either kind of marker pen, as fine as possible for greater accuracy. If the mark is unhelpful, remove it completely or remove part of it using a cotton wool bud. It is not always necessary to mark vertical *and* horizontal lines; decide which will be the most helpful.

Finalising the design

- Make the final decision on the exact words to be used.
- Draw guidelines on layout paper, and indicate clearly the length of line. Guidelines provide a structure in which to work; knowing the restrictions, the calligrapher can write with freedom.
- With a broad felt tipped pen begin working on visual texture (different heights and different thicknesses of stroke) by writing out the letters in several sizes and styles on layout paper. This will provide only an approximate suggestion because the sizes of felt tips are limited. Notice any interesting features which arise during these practice sessions and incorporate them into the writing.

- With an idea of height, weight and style beginning to form, change to double pencils. These can be adjusted to the width of stroke proposed.
- The words should be written and rewritten within the allotted space in the style decided until the rhythm is comfortable and the letter shapes are acceptable. This might take some time. However, the letters must sit comfortably in the space without appearing squashed and they should be formed with confidence and freedom or they will look lifeless.
- If flourishes are to be part of the design, some idea of their position and shape should be considered at this point and noted mentally, but more detailed work on these will come later.

Edward Johnston writes in his *Formal Penmanship*, 'The fact that the broad-nibbed pen produces thick or thin strokes in absolute relation to its direction, distinguishes it from every other tool and enables it to make, out of collections of simple strokes, letters of marked character and finish with the greatest possible regularity and ease'.

If the design for the engraving is based on the broad nib, double pencils can be used to develop rhythm and letterform at the first stage but this writing tool will also provide all the information that is needed for the next stage. The two lines from the double pencils will give the precise positions *for the edges* of every stroke. The images to be engraved are therefore easily visible and can be transferred to the glass with confidence.

Designs based on other writing tools require a further stage of drawing before the letters can be transferred to the glass. The final image is covered with layout paper and the edges of the letters are traced onto this (using the broken line method to retain the original form – see p. 70). Tracing paper is not recommended; compared to layout paper it is unyielding and (despite pressure from the sharp, hard pencil) the wax from the carbon paper will not transfer so well to the surface of the glass.

Planning a monogram

Check the height and width of the area which will allow a comfortable size for the monogram, remembering that the image will disappear around curves at the sides of a straight-sided goblet and also at the top and base of a curving decanter. Draw out this area on a layout pad and use it as a template. Write out the letters so that they are the same height and weight. Cut closely round the images to separate them. Develop the design by moving the images about in different arrangements; place a sheet of layout paper over each new arrangement and re-draw it. Continue to develop the design using this method.

Re-drawing the letters will help to develop observation and practical skill. Because the letters have at first related to each other, if scale and weight are deliberately altered, or if flourishes are included, the basis for development will be sound.

Planning letters in a circle on a horizontal plane

Note the comments in First Questions on p. 50 when designing for discs or wide but shallow bowls. Draw a circle (of appropriate scale) on layout paper with a pair of compasses and use this as a template. Divide up the circle with as many diameter lines as will be helpful; mark the area which is to be used for the lettering. Whatever italic lean is needed can be measured off each diagonal line to give a consistent guide all the way round; use different colours to help with the planning. Whilst developing the design, watch that the letters maintain the direction intended – either upright or with an italic lean. To do this, check the 'visual centre' of each letter with one of the diameter (or italic) lines; a capital 'H', for example, will look wrong if it is lined up on one or the other of its vertical strokes. Most letters will require extremely subtle adjustments to the basic shape.

Although careful geometrical measurement in the early stages of planning the design is necessary, this should ultimately give way to visual judgement.

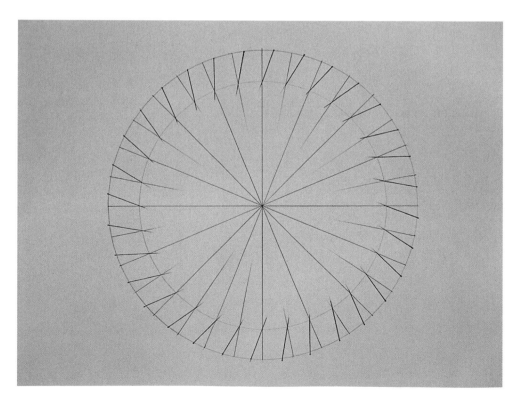

CHAPTER NINE

Transferring the design

A cylindrical or conical shaped glass is recommended for the first attempt because a considerable amount of practical ingenuity will be needed to transfer a design to a more complicated shape. *After burning emotional energy and putting much effort into the design, the transfer of this to the correct position on the glass is critical. It will be very disappointing to view the completed engraving and decide that the image should have been raised or lowered, however minimally.*

Place on the workbench masking tape, scissors, water-based fine felt tip pen, waterproof marker pen (perhaps of a different colour), methylated spirit; facial tissue and/or cotton wool & cotton wool buds, a sharp 5H pencil, and *handwriting* carbon paper. Have a small box, or a selection of thin books available if checking an italic lean (not, at this late stage, to check the drawing, but the positioning of it).

a Make sure the glass is clean. Use either methylated spirit, or a proprietary brand glass cleaner, with an old (non-fluffy) cotton cloth (facial tissues or cotton wool may be used but these tend to leave fibres which sometimes resemble tiny scratches and thus cause alarm); both these substances can be used at the workbench. Alternatively, give the glass a wash in the sink using warm water with washing-up liquid but rinse it thoroughly (otherwise the glass retains an oily deposit) and dry it with an old, clean cloth. Take care that nothing round the sink area will scratch it.

b If there are blemishes (seeds or small scratches which were accepted when the glass was purchased) mark where these are on the inside surface of the glass with the waterproof marker pen. As previously mentioned, a seed will catch the light so will never completely disappear but it may be possible, by carefully positioning the drawing, to engrave over it to reduce its effect.

c Hold the drawing against the glass and make a careful decision on the precise position for the lettering. Except for handmade items, remember to leave at least 12mm/0.47in. space from the rim. With a water-based felt tip marker pen make a small mark on the glass (the smaller, the more accurate) at either the top or the base line of the letters. This will be the location mark when finally fixing the drawing to the glass. Remove the drawing.

d With a water-based marker pen (perhaps of different colour), draw a line round the glass *near but not on the same level as the location mark*

to establish the horizontal. This line will help to position the drawing but will not interfere with either the traced letters or the engraving.

e Vulnerable parts of the glass must now be protected because it will be handled a great deal in many positions during the engraving. Put masking tape over the rim to prevent chipping and on the base to prevent scratching. (Be sure to make the decision about the final position of the lettering *before* the protective tape is put on; even if the tape used is transparent, it will affect visual perception and judgement.)

f Have ready small pieces of masking tape (these are preferable to large which tend to stick where and when they are not wanted). Decide whether these pieces should be attached at the top edge of the drawing or the bottom edge. Snip the paper at top and bottom between letters (not between strokes) to release it. Using the small location mark as a guide, position the drawing and attach it to the glass in one place only with the first piece of masking tape. Check the base line of the lettering with the horizontal guide line and secure the second piece of tape. Work all the way round the glass, continually checking the drawing

Placing the location mark; the best writing has been cut from the layout sheet and trimmed closely.

with the horizontal line. Place the drawing tightly against the glass but relax it very slightly at each piece of tape to allow for the handwriting carbon paper to be slipped behind.

g Cut a small piece of handwriting carbon paper and slide this beneath the drawing. To transfer the drawing, use a hard pencil – at least a 5H – sharpened to a fine point. Do not re-draw the letters with a solid line because this can lose the original shape. Mark the letters with small short lines following the flow of the writing movement; mark each side of the pen line from start to finish; this will help to retain the movement and also to keep the crossover points crisp. Extreme accuracy is necessary because the character of a letter can be subtly changed by increasing or decreasing the shape or width of strokes by as little as the width of a fine pencil line. Move the carbon paper along until all the letters have been transferred. Before removing the drawing, look *inside* the glass where the wax marks from the handwriting carbon paper should be clearly visible; check that every part of each letter has been transferred.

If something is not right, be brave! Remove the drawing carefully, wipe off the carbon marks, reposition the design, and begin again. Because the drawing was transferred with small,

Drawing in position and glass protected at the rim and around the edge of the foot. Note releasing snips in the paper.

short lines on the first occasion, the original letter shapes can still be clearly seen. Place the 5H pencil in these *same marks* – do not create any new ones – and transfer the design to the glass as before. This method allows the original design always to remain visible; it can therefore be used for yet another try, or if the glass is broken and the design needs to be repeated at a later date.

Comment

When the drawing has been removed, be careful not to smudge the carbon marks. Decide on the position where the engraving will begin and, if there is a risk that any handling, or movement on the cushion, will accidentally rub off some of the tracing, place a clean piece of layout paper over the glass on the vulnerable area; attach it firmly with masking tape because, if this moves about, it will also cause smudging.

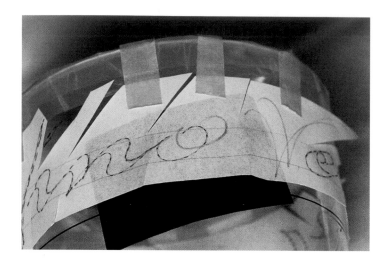

The letters marked with small, short or dotted lines which follow the flow of the writing movement. The shapes of the written letters remain clearly visible.

All the lettering traced onto the goblet.

Engraving the design

Whether working 'wet' or 'dry', engraving can begin in any position. Keep the drawing to hand during the engraving but file it when the work is completed. The wax from the handwriting carbon is particularly vulnerable in hot weather. To avoid smudging the letters, plan the sequence so that neither fingers, nor resting the glass on the support, will erase any of the image. When engraving by the 'dry' method, if protective paper has been placed round one side of the glass, this can be removed when it is no longer serving any purpose. If a letter is smudged during the engraving, do nothing with it until the letters on either side of it have been engraved completely and 'finished'. Then, using these engraved letters as a key, reposition the drawing accurately and re-trace the missing letter in its precise position.

The 'dry' method
The tools needed are: drill; selection of burs; cushion with a covering of

dark coloured material on which to rest the glass (or dark coloured material to place over the cushion); a small, clean dry paint brush. The engraver will need: face mask; eye protection; enlarging visor (if required).

The 'wet' method
For this, the engraver will need the items above (except the small paint brush) and also: one large tray on the workbench in which to gather the water; a container for the water which is raised above the engraving (a plastic ice cream container set on a high shelf, or a plastic bottle suspended from a support above, will do); a narrow tube from the container to a few inches above the work with small (beer making) tap to regulate the flow. To support the glass, use either a black plastic mat or a plastic plate rack (sold for use on a draining board) which will sit in the tray. (This support can also be covered with a dark cloth but wash the cloth and

leave it to dry out after use.) Place a small mirror in the tray so that light can be directed onto the area of engraving. The water supply will need to be topped up frequently and the tray will need to be emptied regularly. Any reference marks on the glass, or when flourishes are drawn, will need to be made with the spirit-based felt tip pen.

Surface engraving technique

The following sequence describes the 'dry' method of engraving. The aim is to achieve an even, opaque texture over the whole of the engraved area; the design should attract the viewer, not how it has been engraved.

To see the traced marks easily, place a white, or light coloured, temporary covering over the supporting cushion (a sheet of A4 paper will do). After the letters have been marked in, it is removed.

A spherical, diamond encrusted bur is recommended for surface engraving. This bur is like a miniature cudgel; it is the diamonds which cut the glass so the bur should not be moved too quickly over it – the diamonds must be given time to cut the surface. (For example, a vacuum cleaner will only collect bits from a carpet provided that the brush is given sufficient time to revolve over a particular area.)

The drill should not run fast. If it does, the bur will tear into the surface and go too deeply into it. The touch must be light at all times. A new bur will mark the glass easily

and precisely. The opaque texture is built up gradually; move the bur gently over the surface in a series of slow 'scribbles'. As it revolves, the bur abrades the surface of the glass and leaves a series of unsightly scratches. Do not work in one area for too long but extend the scratches, returning to 'scribble' over previous areas until an overall, even texture is produced. This is where, for a first attempt, the idea of selecting only a few letters to engrave will be appreciated! Use the soft paint brush to brush away glass dust; this dust can adhere to the wax marks and make other letters look engraved when they are not.

Glass has a slight 'skin' which occurs during manufacture and once this has been abraded it is very easy to go deeper without intending to. Continue working lightly over all the letters and try to keep every one at a similar stage. The diamonds will eventually lose their sharpness. When the bur does not seem to be cutting, it is time to change it. Resist the temptation to press harder because this will cause the bur to make a furrow. Although the worn diamonds will no longer cut the surface of clear glass, the same bur can be used to smooth over areas which have already been abraded and this will help to produce a beautiful, silvery finish.

In whichever area you are working, always turn the glass to the most comfortable position for your hand, even if this means turning the glass upside down. For greater control, move the bur towards rather than away from you. When engraving into corners, use the 'equator' of the bur and turn the glass so that the bur revolves into the area already abraded – not away from it towards the clear glass.

Suggested stages of engraving:
1 the outline of every letter is marked precisely on the glass;
2 all the letters are engraved until there is an even texture over each stroke except at the extreme out side edges;
3 edges, serifs, and crossover points are 'finished';
4 flourishes are designed on the glass, and engraved.

1 With a spherical bur of the smallest diameter, mark in every outline of the design, but avoid serifs and crossover points. Make these marks on the carbon marks. Carefully follow the direction of the drawn line in a series of dots, or very short lines, using the 'equator' of the bur. This can be done fairly rapidly (contrary to expectations) and more quickly than making a continuous line; it helps in keeping a light touch, and one small mark out of place is easier to disregard at a later stage than a solid line. Let the movement of the hand follow the shape of the stroke; the pace of the hand movement as it makes the marks will help to keep the line true and the sharp bur will mark the glass instantly, allowing the

1 Against a temporary, light coloured background, the traced marks from the carbon paper are easily visible. The engraved mark of the bur can be seen against the dark background. Areas from where flourishes may spring are marked in red – to be 'finished' later.

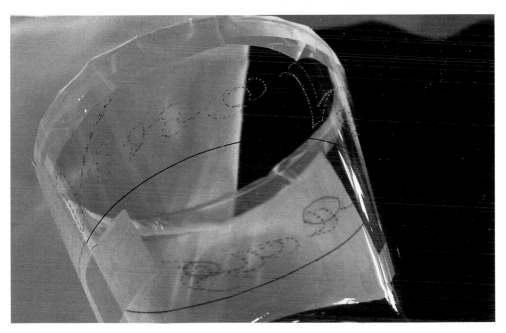

During stage **2**; texture to be improved.

engraver to concentrate on making a good line. For crossover points, follow the *inner side* of the stroke to the outer side (this will help to keep the shape of the crossover point) but avoid, for the moment, marking the glass at the precise crossover point.

2 Shade in every letter to begin the build up of overall texture, continuing to use a slow, gentle 'scribble' movement over the surface. Change to a new bur whenever necessary; if the glass is hard, this will need to be more often than if working on crystal. If the letter strokes are wide, change to a larger sphere in order to cover the area more quickly but continue to maintain a light touch – with a larger bur it is easier to make accidental furrows. Work over the

whole design until the required texture is the same on every letter. Go as close to the edges of letters as possible but be particularly careful when using a larger bur.

Stage 2 completed.

3 Using a new, smallest size bur, tidy edges, draw in serifs (the position of these might have altered slightly) and complete all crossover points. One or two touches of the bur (as if re-touching a photograph) on the unengraved parts of the edges will produce an apparently straight line;

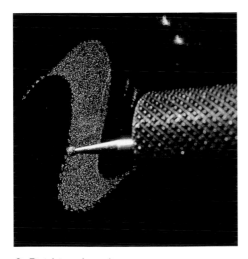

3 Finishing the edges.

the closer the initial marks were made to each other in Stage 1 the quicker this can be done. Blend in the effect of the edge engraving with the body of the stroke by more light 'scribbling'.

4 Finalise designs of flourishes on the glass with a marker pen (use spirit-based pens when working 'wet'). Check the effect of the proposed flourish from various positions. If there are to be two or more, watch how they relate to each other *through* the glass. Engrave them using either a new, smallest size spherical bur or a new, tapered bur (a rat tail) but with the latter, be very careful not to go *into* the glass.

Flourishes

Designs of flourishes will depend on the original writing tool on which the design is based, the shape of the glass, and the amount of space available. The broad nib can produce a monoline – as if it were tilted onto one or the other of its 'corners'; or it can make a flourish the same weight as the letters, or a different effect can be produced by drawing a flourish as though it had been made using a narrower broad nib. Copperplate-based designs particularly lend themselves to flourishes. Whatever the design, the flourish should never distort the original shape of the letter. A flourish should not appear to be added on but should develop from the mark made by the writing tool as it either moves into, or out of, the letter.

Flourishes should either flow (with vigour), or look like a cracking whip or an expertly cast fishing line. However, if the designs for these are worked out on layout paper and then transferred, their visual energy which provides so much drama in a piece of work can be killed by curves in the glass. It is better to draw them spontaneously on to the glass.

Designing a flourish

After the lettering has been engraved, plan the movement of the flourishes on layout paper bearing in mind how the writing tool would move and the area available for the flourish. Then repeat this movement on the glass using a dark coloured felt tip pen. This may take some time. Remove each unwanted mark quickly – too many lines in a similar area are confusing so it is better to remove the result of each attempt. Continue until a satisfactory shape appears.

Engraving a flourish

To mark the glass, use either the equator of a spherical bur or a tapered bur. Place the mark precisely in the centre of the line. As soon as the bur touches the glass, the white mark it makes will be seen clearly against the dark line from the felt tip. Follow the movement of the line carefully. Any swelling in the line is added gradually, taking care to engrave this so that it relates to the movement and shape made by whichever writing tool was used for the design.

4 Marking in the flourish.

Whilst engraving the flourish, if the bur moves off the marked line, stop immediately. It might be possible to rescue the shape of the line but, to retain the movement of a good flourish, it may be necessary to terminate the line in a different place – and sooner than planned.

When the engraving is finished, wash the glass carefully and put it in a safe place.

Comments

• Although it is not vital, during the engraving the glass might benefit from being cleaned; it becomes covered with finger marks and glass dust, which may scratch it, and the gentle cleaning provides a break in concentration and permits an appraisal of progress. Because the edges of all the letters have been engraved accurately with the bur, the removal of any remaining carbon marks will not matter. Use methylated spirit at the workbench (do not rub the glass but 'lift' the dust away with cotton wool) or put it under running water at the kitchen sink with washing-up liquid, taking care as before.

- Maintain in mind the intended letterform. If the engraving departs from the traced marks, concentrate on the letter which is emerging and develop it correctly by further exercises with the writing tool, so keep this and the layout pad within easy reach.

- During the engraving, shake the cushion cover frequently. It will become impregnated with glass dust and, as the object is turned and moved about during the engraving, the dust can scratch it. Hours of work could be ruined in the final few minutes.

- An advantage in engraving lettering on glass is that, if there are interruptions, work can stop immediately and be resumed again at any time without loss of 'writing' rhythm.

Mistakes

Glass engravers who work on subjects other than lettering can incorporate accidental marks from the bur into their design without too much anguish. This is rarely the case when working with letters.

Accidents can happen at any time. If the engraver is not familiar with an enlarging visor, this can cause the bur to make contact with the glass before the engraver is ready! Or, after a brief interval for appraisal or to answer the telephone, a multi-radial surface can also disorientate for a split second – and the damage is done.

It is possible to remove unwanted marks by 'polishing' them out. This involves many stages of work over the problem area using a series of fine grits, followed by felt burs impregnated with polishing powders to bring the surface to its original sheen – 'back to black'. This can take a very long time, particularly if the mark is deep. It might be a better use of time to begin again on another glass, but this will need to be judged against the cost. Because the profile of the surface is changed, the area of correction will be noticed if the light catches the glass at a particular angle.

The engraving completed including flourish.

The Ribbon Goblet.
The flourish has been partly drill engraved and partly stipple engraved to provide contrasting textures.

CHAPTER ELEVEN

Presentation

The glass should be spotless when it is presented. Hands, however clean, contain natural oils which will leave finger marks on the glass. During the presentation, there has to be a balance between holding the glass so that it is not dropped and ensuring that it remains clean. The best way to overcome this, after giving the glass a final clean, is to wear cotton gloves to place the item in a presentation box.

Specialist firms make inexpensive boxes in a variety of sizes that contain a certain amount of padding and have attractive linings – but they are not very robust. An alternative would be to have a box custom-made, but padding and lining must be considered.

If possible, arrange that the recipient will not have an embarrassing struggle to extricate the glass from its container during the presentation. An alternative idea to offering the glass in a presentation box might be to place it in advance on a table, on a dark cloth. (It can be carefully boxed later.) If other people are attending, they will have the opportunity to view and examine the work before it is presented. The glass can, if it is thought appropriate, be covered before the presentation.

Presentation boxes should not be sent through the post without further packaging (see p. 100).

Sandblast

Commercial sandblasting has given this method a poor reputation but, combined with good design and the skill of experienced operators, it can provide either a useful alternative to hand engraving or can be combined with it. If an engraver owns, or has access to, a sandblast cabinet this can also influence the solution of the final design. Some technical colleges make their facilities available for hire. Masks can be originated by the engraver (see p. 81) or stencils can be made by a specialist company from artwork provided by the engraver. Large areas of glass such as windows, doors, screens and panels, are more often sandblasted than hand engraved. A panel might be partly sandblasted commercially and then further work will be done by the engraver; thus the somewhat bland result of sandblast is supplemented by interesting effects produced by the use of drill and bur.

Sandblast cabinet

Small cabinets can be purchased by the individual engraver from suppliers listed in the telephone directory. This will entail considerable financial outlay because, apart from the cabinet, a compressor, a dust extractor, and a supply of grit, will be needed. Siting all this equipment and storing the grit will require a certain amount of space; the safe disposal of dust must also be considered. Maintenance should be carried out regularly by the engraver or by a specialist company.

Grit

Companies that supply abrasives will be found in the telephone directory. The engraver will need to decide what kind of grit, and what grade, to use; finer grades (the higher numbers) will be more expensive. Abrasive grit is usually sold in minimum quantities of 25kg/55lb. A variety of grits are available but white alumina is the hardest and sharpest; it provides a 'soft' white finish.

The finest grit will be needed to cut the smallest letters successfully; it will also provide a good edge to letters of any size and leave a smooth 'white' surface. If a more textured surface is required, a coarser grit should be used. When producing designs with areas of different textures, the engraver must replace the grit in the cabinet for each grade. The finest grit should be used first, then subsequent grades, finishing with the coarsest. (See p. 96).

Renewal of grit

During the sandblast process, the grit is recycled within the sandblast cabinet; however, because some will be lost to the dust extractor, the hopper in the base of the cabinet will need to be topped up occasionally. It is not possible to state how quickly the grit will lose its cutting power; this will depend on how often, and for how long, it is used and also the hardness of the glass. Eventually, more will have to be ordered from the suppliers.

Masks for sandblast

To protect the areas which are to remain clear, the glass needs to be covered with a resist which is able to withstand the effect of an abrasive grit fired at pressure for a certain length of time.

Masks made by the engraver:

For a simple design which is to be surface engraved, the engraver can use masking tape and cut the design through this. Also, see caption on p. 41. A more robust protection is provided by adhesive-backed plastic, available from most DIY or hardware stores.

Commercially made masks:

Alternatively, the engraver can use masks or stencils which are made by commercial companies who can provide different kinds and are pleased to advise on the one which will be suitable for the task in hand.

The most usual commercially made masks are: *printed tissue stencil, gummed paper stencil, direct film stencil,* and *vinyl stencil.* Where an adhesive is needed, this will be supplied with the stencil and with detailed directions for use. For the first three, the image is reproduced photographically so can be enlarged or reduced from the original artwork as required; for the fourth, artwork is scanned by a computer so the image can also be re-sized. However, it is always advisable to work to the size of the finished article or as closely as possible to it so that adjustments during the reproduction process are minimal. Even photocopying a drawing at the same size can result in small distortions.

Printed tissue stencils: the emulsion is prepared with a thin support paper. The stencil is fixed to the glass with either an aerosol adhesive or with water-soluble gum. The thin tissue will adjust to multi-radial surfaces, but is difficult to apply to large areas.

81

Gummed paper stencils: these are ink stencils printed on paper with a gum coating on the reverse, rather like a postage stamp. More robust than tissue, the paper is easier to handle so is more suitable for large areas; this stencil allows for deeper blasting, but is almost impossible to apply to multi-radial surfaces.

Direct film stencils: these are made from a light-sensitive emulsion without a backing and are covered with a 'support layer' of flexible lacquer which must be removed carefully before sandblasting begins to avoid dislodging centres of letters. These stencils will cope with multi-radial surfaces. With no paper to pierce, the grit blasting is instant. (This method can cope with the finest detail so, with a fine grade of grit, is used to reproduce half-tone illustrations.)

Vinyl stencils: these are cut from self-adhesive plastic sheet by a computer-guided blade. The vinyl is covered by a support paper; once attached to the glass this support paper is removed carefully (as above). This heavy-duty material provides stencils which allow a considerable depth of blasting. Because of the method of cutting, the edges of italic letters tend to look like the blade of a miniature saw, so it is preferable to use it only for bold designs on a large scale. This material cannot be applied to multi-radial surfaces.

Peter Furlonger
Lux in tenebris lucet
Bowl, diameter 115mm/4.52in., with hard-wood base. The glass is covered with self-adhesive plastic and the design is handcut through this; the glass is then sandblasted. Base and glass are 'not fixed together, the base being an afterthought which immediately became an integral element in the overall design. Hence, the base remains in a permanent relationship to the bowl'. The piece is a result of a chance encounter that has since become a working principle for the engraver who believes that 'accidents are points of departure for new discoveries'.

CHAPTER THIRTEEN

Design considerations for sandblast

Because sandblasting can be used for surface engraving and for any depth of blasting, and different grades of grit can be used to give different textures, there are several avenues to exploit. As with drill engraving, there is a choice between engraving the letters or engraving the background. It is much quicker to cut away deeply using the sandblast method than by using the drill.

When designing letters to be hand-cut from self-adhesive plastic which has already been applied to the glass, another tool, the knife, will have an influence on the shape of the letter. Any practical problems in the cutting must be borne in mind and perhaps a compromise made in the design; for instance, very tight curves on serif brackets might be difficult to cut so will make a tight, uncomfortable looking shape. Ideally, the knife should be able to follow the letter on the drawing without a problem; if the blade moves off this line, *the*

movement of the hand must continue without trying to regain the original line. The shape of the cut letter might therefore differ slightly from the drawn one but this is preferable to an awkward shape where the engraver has tried to correct the line.

Attempting to cut small letters as reproductions of those made by a pen or from type is aesthetically unsatisfactory and a waste of energy; if this is what is required, then a commercially made stencil should be used.

How the work is to be produced will influence decisions about what kind of mask or stencil is the most suitable; for example, the design might combine a hand-cut mask and a commercially made stencil. If this is the case, prudence suggests that they might be sandblasted one at a time; the engraver must therefore plan the sequence of work. If the design calls for different depths, the deeper letters should be engraved first.

Comments

- For a hand cut design which is to be deeply blasted, apply a second, or third layer of self-adhesive plastic to the glass before cutting.
- A clear and precise drawing should be prepared before it is secured to the plastic. Hesitant cut marks due to a vague drawing will be obvious when the blasting has been done. Confident cutting will have a character of its own and be apparent in the finished work.
- Unless the letters are of great scale, and intended to be seen from a distance, avoid using a *vinyl* stencil for a design which features an italic letter (see p. 83).

Hand cut mask: attaching self-adhesive plastic

It is simple to transfer a design for sandblast to a flat surface so, for a first attempt, choose a small pane of glass, or a cylindrical beaker. Most suppliers of self-adhesive plastic will cut lengths from a roll which may be as narrow as 100mm/3.9in. and, depending on the size of the design, this might be sufficient for a first try.

EPH Glass block, 80 x 80 x 60mm/3.14 x 3.14 x 2.36in. This birthday paperweight was engraved with the initials of the recipient. The fact that he preferred, and was known to friends by, his second name, formed the basis of the design. A hand cut mask was sand blasted to give a slight edge to the smaller letters, and more deeply for a greater edge on the 'P'. On the right hand vertical plane near the top edge, the personal message was directly written extremely small with a drill using a tapered bur running slowly. The refractions are, again, intriguing.

Although easily applied, the plastic must not be stretched. It can also be used on curved vessels, again without stretching it, but cutting on a curved surface is more difficult and best left until more experience has been gained. Where joins are necessary, the plastic should overlap by 2mm/0.078in. at least and work should be planned so that the knife blade will not pass through these; likewise any wrinkles on curved surfaces will be quite safe provided they are not cut.

Before attaching the plastic, the surface to be engraved should be thoroughly cleaned with either a spirit-based cleaner or washing up liquid and rinsed.

Covering a small pane of glass
Either cover the whole pane of glass with the plastic, or, only the area round the lettering. Other protective material, like masking tape, can be used over the remaining areas which will not be subjected to the blast.

Covering a larger area
If covering a large area (for example, 500mm square/19.5 in, square) the following procedure may be helpful: It is preferable to remove the backing paper in small quantities because large areas of flapping plastic with exposed adhesive are difficult to control – the width of the strips suggested is only a guide.
a Position the plastic correctly and decide which area should be attached to the glass first.

b Move to the opposite end of the plastic and secure this with masking tape; this is a temporary measure to prevent it moving out of position before the next stage.
c Where the plastic is to be first attached, peel away and cut off a small strip (not more than 100mm/3.9in. wide) of the backing paper. Do not let the exposed adhesive touch anything. Wait about ten seconds to allow the plastic to relax. (If it sticks on the surface in a stretched condition the cutting, which will make the plastic 'give', could result in a distorted letter.) From the direction of the masking tape, smooth the plastic down gently on the glass surface without stretching it and, if there are no trapped air bubbles, it can be rubbed down securely.
d Remove and discard the masking tape which will have served its purpose.
e Peel away another 100mm/3.9in. of backing paper and cut it off. Support the area of unprotected adhesive and, as before, do not allow it to touch anything; pause for at least ten seconds to let it 'relax'. Then, again without stretching it, gently rub the plastic down; if there are no trapped air bubbles, rub it down securely.
f Repeat until the glass has been covered.

Comments
- However carefully the plastic is laid, trapped air bubbles often

develop. It will depend on the design as to how much they will be a nuisance. If they are fairly small they can be ignored. Large ones will be noticed as the plastic is gently smoothed down and it is possible to reduce the size, if not completely to remove them, by swiftly lifting the plastic, again letting it relax, and then laying it once more. Often the best plan is to wait until the design has been attached and then decide the best way to treat any bubbles which might cause problems.

- It is not necessary to prick a bubble if the knife blade will not pass through it. If it will, make sure the edge of that letter is securely attached to the glass.
- If you wish to burst the bubble, hold the blade almost parallel to the surface as you cut to avoid marking the glass with the blade. Cut a fresh piece of plastic and stick this over the break in the surface. Bear in mind that in the sandblast cabinet considerable pressure directed at a small piece of plastic could blast it away so make sure any extra pieces adhere firmly. (These must be checked regularly during the sandblasting process to make sure they are not lifting.)

Attaching a commercially made vinyl mask

Follow the sequence from **a** – **f** above. When the vinyl mask is finally in place, carefully peel off the covering support paper and remove the pre-cut letters. A vinyl mask is made from a heavier material than self adhesive plastic so it should go down onto the surface with little risk of bubbles; the 'Comments' section above should not apply. When placing the order, enquire about extra masks in case of mishaps. Also, assuming it is the letters which are to be sandblasted, discuss whether the supplier will remove these or leave them in place beneath the support paper for the engraver to remove. It is preferable for the engraver to do this because removing the letters can be time consuming and needs to be done with care – particularly if they are small when counters of lowercase 'a' and 'e' can come adrift. They can be pressed firmly back into position but will need to be checked during sandblasting.

Hand cut mask: attaching the drawing

Always take a photocopy of the final design and file it. Two methods, using either a spray glue or rubber based adhesive, for attaching the drawing to the self-adhesive plastic are suggested. If designs need to be reversed/flipped the letters will be seen fairly clearly through the layout paper once it is stuck on the plastic; alternatively, retrace the letters on the reverse side of the layout paper over a light box or, if this is unavailable, tape the drawing to a window. The seeming tedium of having to re-draw the image is counterbalanced by the advantage gained by yet more drawing.

Spray glue

A permanent spray glue, used according to the directions on the container, will provide excellent adhesion; this will not permit re-positioning of the drawing. A spray glue which allows re-positioning is more useful. However, with either of these spray glues, once in the cabinet, small particles of drawing paper which are worn and then detached from the plastic by the sandblast process can be re-circulated in the cabinet and returned to the hopper; when the grit is drawn up into the supply tube to the gun these particles can block the nozzle of the gun. Work will be delayed while the blockage is removed.

Rubber-based adhesive

This is applied to the self adhesive plastic with a spreader (or fingers) and the drawing placed on top. This method permits adjustment of the drawing but does not provide quite such thorough adhesion as the spray glues. Care is therefore needed during cutting to make sure the drawing stays in place; if some areas become unstuck, more glue can easily be applied where and when necessary. The advantage with this adhesive is that, when the letters have been cut out, the drawing paper remaining on the plastic can be peeled off it and discarded before the glass is placed in the sandblast cabinet.

Suggested procedure:

1 Position the drawing correctly.

2 Attach it in one place with masking tape.
3 Using the masking tape as a hinge, fold back the drawing so it is out of the way; cover it to protect it with a spare sheet of paper whilst the glue (of whichever kind) is applied to the upper surface of the plastic.
4 From the direction of the masking tape, smooth the drawing onto the plastic making sure that it goes down without any wrinkles. Place a spare sheet of paper over the drawing to protect it and rub it down securely.

Attaching commercially made stencils *(see illustrations a – g)*

The method described above can be equally applied to attaching commercially made stencils to the glass surface. The companies who supply these stencils will usually provide a few extra in case of mishaps; these are fairly delicate, particularly during spraying and fixing to the glass. Follow the same sequence as attach-

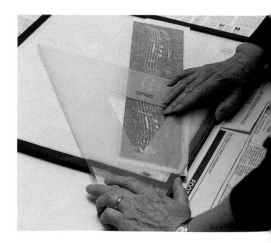

a Positioning the stencil

b Forming 'hinges' for each stencil with masking tape

e From the 'hinge', laying down the first stencil

c 'Hinged' stencil laid aside

f Laying down the remaining stencil

d Spraying the cleaned glass with adhesive

g Ensuring good adhesion

An opportunity to use engraved lettering on glass to its fullest. A new music school commissioned viewing panels for eighteen internal doors, 400mm/15.8 in. square. Each panel bears the surname of a composer with a few bars of well known music. The director of music requested that time signatures were omitted so that successive generations of pupils could work out the rhythm for themselves. Names of composers were originated with large nibs of different sizes (see p. 56) held at different angles and were written in different styles; Bach had to work well in the same space as Shostakovich. In addition, the client accepted the idea to include Christian names and dates of birth and death; these are superimposed and half superimposed through the surname. The 'flourish' of the musical staves were different for each composer except for two. They were developed using the five-nib calligraphic pen and enlarged by photo copying.

Shortness of time caused all the 'music' stencils to be made before all the 'composers' so each pair had to be married on the glass; this was an advantage because the sizes of the stencils were easier to handle than they might have been.

ing the drawing to the plastic when using the *spray adhesive*. Finally, with an old, dry toothbrush, rub down the whole area carefully but thoroughly to ensure complete adhesion.

Cutting the design

Always take a fresh scalpel blade; a blunt blade will pucker the plastic and the drawing paper. It is a matter of personal choice which shape of blade to use. Straight lines are generally cut with a straight blade, curved ones with a curved blade, and small curved lines with a small curved blade. (Similarly, the wheel engraver must select the appropriate circumference of wheel for the curve required, so must change to the appropriate size of wheel as the size of the curve changes.) If there is much cutting to be done, make sure there is a good supply of the different shapes of blade. At every stage of cutting, the blade must be kept at a right angle to the surface.

It is possible to develop a rhythm when cutting as it is when writing. Cover a spare piece of glass with plastic and also with a layer of paper of the same quality as that used for the drawing. Make a few practice strokes to see how it feels to cut through the materials; the paper provides an excellent 'key' for the blade. (It is more difficult to control the blade when cutting directly onto plastic – as it is to control a writing tool on a shiny surface.) There is no need to press hard because a new blade will cut easily; it is only the

A variety of blades in different holders; the round grip is preferable for cutting many, and large, letters.

paper and plastic which need to be cut. Too much pressure could damage the surface of the glass and thus spoil the edge of the letter; this mistake will always be visible because, being a different texture, it will reflect the light differently from the rest of the word.

a Turn the work so that cutting can be done in the most comfortable position; if it is a large piece of glass, move into a position where **b** can be accomplished without losing balance and/or overstretching.

b Always cut through the layers of plastic and paper with one stroke; re-cutting is possible if done carefully with no extra pressure but it tends to spoil both rhythm and confidence. Each cut should flow

The knife should be kept at a right angle to the surface.

with one movement; any hesitation and minute change of direction might be revealed in the final sandblasting.

c Where one stroke crosses another on the drawing, do *not cut* where these cross; make the one movement as above but, at the precise moment when the blade reaches the cross bar, take off the pressure, continue the movement, then re-engage the blade as the stroke re-emerges from the crossbar and continue cutting to the end. If the blade cuts into the area to be blasted, the nature of sandblast will cause the mark of the blade to be continued down into the glass always just a little deeper than the grit, so it will never disappear. (For this reason, once cutting has begun it is not possible to remove all the plastic, re-cover, and begin work again on the same piece of glass.)

d Take the cut to the exact end of the drawn line and no further. Do not overcut; a sharp blade will make a mark even on hard (plate) glass.

e If you need to change blades when cutting a curve which tightens, lift the blade away gently and with the new blade, re-enter the exact place gently; *continue the same movement* and complete the cut.

f Peel away unwanted plastic slowly. If this is pulled away carelessly and has not been properly cut, it could not only stretch but may also tear the immediate area. Re-cut any corners by sliding the blade gently into the previous mark made by it, remembering that only the plastic needs to be cut.

g Any excess adhesive which has not pulled away with the plastic from the areas to be sandblasted must be removed. If left on, this could become an effective barrier to the grit. Use the tip of a cocktail stick to gather it up; for more stubborn particles, slightly dampen the tip. Do not use a solvent or saturate the surface with water (after sandblasting, the self-adhesive plastic will be washed off the glass with water!). If any rubber-based adhesive has crept onto these areas, it can be lifted off by pressing it, carefully, with a dried piece of the same, or with the cocktail stick, or with the tip of the blade.

Comments
- In hot weather the adhesive on the back of the plastic can become very 'treacly'. As unwanted plastic is peeled away, the adhesive trails along the edge of the cut and can be difficult to remove from the surface of the glass. The result is a less than clean edge to the letter; the remedy is to leave the plastic for a while in the refrigerator before using it. (This situation could be exploited on another project experimenting with texture.)
- If an edge of the letter is marred during cutting, take a small piece

After the letters are cut the glass must be scrutinised with a magnifier to ensure that the surface to be blasted is completely clear of any glue or other debris.

of plastic large enough to cover the area and, away from the glass, re-cut this to the correct shape (this could take some time). Remove the backing paper and wait for the plastic to relax. Stick it securely over the incorrect edge; make sure that no grit will be able to penetrate under the joined layers.

Protecting the glass

After the design has been cut out and the surface to be sandblasted exposed, the rest of the glass will need to be protected from the grit. Depending on the size of the glass, cover it either with more self adhesive plastic, or wide masking tape, or several layers of newspaper. Whatever material is used, look carefully at every join (holding the glass up to the light will help) to make sure there are no areas of clear glass which have been missed. Under pressure, a fine grit will penetrate a pin hole.

Cutting for deep sandblasting

The nature of plastic provides a good protection from sandblast because it causes the grit to bounce off it rather than allowing the grit to cut into it. One layer of self-adhesive plastic will withstand considerable use but for confidence when intending to sand-blast deeply, cover the glass with two layers of plastic, applying first one layer to the glass surface then the other. Cutting will not be more difficult but, again, a little practice will help to get the feel of the blade through the drawing paper and the layers of plastic. Make sure that the cut goes through *all the layers at the same time.*

CHAPTER FOURTEEN

In the sandblast cabinet

Below are suggestions for preliminary tests in a small workshop situation. Commercial sandblasting is on a different scale but the principles are the same.

Take a piece of plate glass measuring approximately 140 x 250mm/ 5.51in. x 9.84in; cover it with plastic; in two rows of four, cut eight 40mm/1.57in. squares in the plastic; remove only the first square to reveal the glass. Each of these will be treated differently. Once each square has been sandblasted, recover it with masking tape.

Testing with different times: using a low pressure, blast the first square for a few seconds; cover it; remove the second square and blast this for slightly longer; cover this also. Continue, lengthening the time of exposure to the grit, until four squares have been blasted.

Testing with different pressures (psi; pounds per square inch): using the

remaining four squares, keep the time the same for each, but increase the pressure for each and cover each after it has been blasted. Remove the plastic under a running tap. Drill engrave the relevant details beneath each square for future reference.

Working practice:

- Rest the glass on a plastic mat (the open kind used for sink or draining board) to protect it from the metal grid in the cabinet.
- The gun should be moved constantly and held no closer than 70mm/2.75in. from the surface of the glass.
- The grit should hit the glass at a right angle; but be aware that because of the trajectory effect, this will not be the case round the perimeter of the blast.
- Move the gun in a circular pattern to avoid any pauses in the action (which will carve a dip in the surface). It may also be moved vertically and horizontally in a regular

pattern provided the 'ends' of the movements go beyond the glass onto the plastic.

- Maintaining the gun at a right angle is not difficult on a flat plane but care should be taken to continue this when the gun is moved round a curved glass vessel; force from an oblique angle could drive grit beneath the edge of the mask.
- Make regular checks on the progress of the blasting by removing the item from the cabinet and scrutinising it carefully in a good light. Looking at the surface through a magnifying glass will help.
- Check that any extra patches of plastic are continuing to adhere securely. If they are not, either stop to remove them and stick on more (first, wiping as much grit from the surface as possible) or, cease working in that area.
- When blasting more deeply and a straight, downward cut is wanted to the edge of a letter, begin with and maintain a low pressure; a high pressure will make a curved profile.

Sandblasting with different grits

When producing designs using different textures, the engraver must change the grit in the cabinet for each grade. The finest grade should be used first, then subsequent grades, finishing with the coarsest. This will

entail thoroughly cleaning out the previous grade not only from the cabinet, but also from the hopper, from the supply tube, and from the gun. Areas of the design already blasted will need to be protected from each subsequent blasting so work should be planned accordingly.

Cleaning up

When the blasting is completed, all the protective materials must be peeled away from the glass under a running tap because grit can still scratch the glass. If this is done at the kitchen sink, do this with the plug in place. When the glass is free of all its protection, dry it and set it aside on a clean cloth or a paper towel. Remove as much of the debris from the sink as possible and wrap it in newspaper. Tilt the plug very slightly and let the water drain away very slowly. The small amount of residual grit in the sink may now be removed with a handful of kitchen paper towel, wrapped in newspaper and disposed of safely.

Photographing engraved lettering

Photography is an art form in itself and photographing glass is one subject in a vast field. It is difficult to photograph glass and even more difficult to photograph engraved lettering. A few brief points might help to avoid pitfalls and disappointments.

Professional photographer

Make sure the photographer knows a little about glass from a practical point of view; for example, that full lead, or lead crystal, will scratch easily. (There is a story that, for a special effect, the delicate work of one engraver was placed against a brick wall.) Specify the area which should be the main subject and the preferred height of the camera. Be certain about the visual effect you require; because the eye naturally compensates, all engraved lettering will be in focus when seen with the naked eye. The camera will not automatically compensate; the exposure must be adjusted. In a print, lettering out of focus can be disconcerting because that is not how it is naturally seen.

Photography by the engraver

Although a good professional photograph will provide a record for the engraver, be a reference for clients and be useful for reproduction in publicity material, it will involve expense. An alternative is for the engraver to photograph the work. To set up an impromptu studio; place a table against a wall and attach a large sheet of plain paper (of appropriate colour) to the wall, high enough to provide a backdrop, and allow the paper to curve down to cover the table. The camera should be close enough to the subject so that the edges of the paper are not seen through the viewfinder. This ensures that there will be no other visual distractions within shot. Position the glass on this. A single lens reflex camera will provide the necessary flexibility in exposure and focussing. The camera must always be rigid so

97

place it on a tripod or other solid structure.

Decide whether to use daylight or artificial light; if the latter, wait until evening so that windows do not have to be blacked out. Taking photographs by natural light can cause problems; it might never come from the correct direction and items in the room may be reflected in the glass. Strong sunlight can create difficulties. With artificial light, the source can be a spotlight, halogen light or desk lamp; unless using black and white film, obtain a blue daylight correction filter from any photographic shop; wear dark coloured clothing and keep well away from the glass whilst the shot is being taken. How the lighting will be directed will depend entirely on the shape of the glass and where the lettering appears on it (the same shape of glass with lettering engraved within a different area will require a different lighting).

Take time to compose the picture

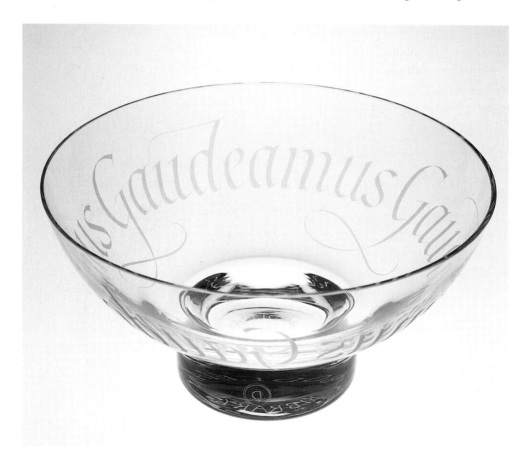

Freddie Quartley
Presentation Bowl. Dartington crystal, diameter 230 mm/7.08in. The drill engraved lettering repeats the traditional Latin 'Gaudeamus'. For the Bodleian Library, University of Oxford. Photograph by Dick Makin.

well. (For an audience, a series of slides or photographs becomes very tedious viewing when objects are not level or where irrelevant space distracts in every shot.) Check that the letters are seen together in the desired effect. Take a series of shots with various exposures.

Always take several pictures of the same view; these will always be useful for sending to prospective clients, galleries, and other organisations (who might keep them for a long time or may never return them) and it is less expensive than having copies made.

However well photographed, a two-dimensional illustration will never be able to do justice to a piece of engraved glass.

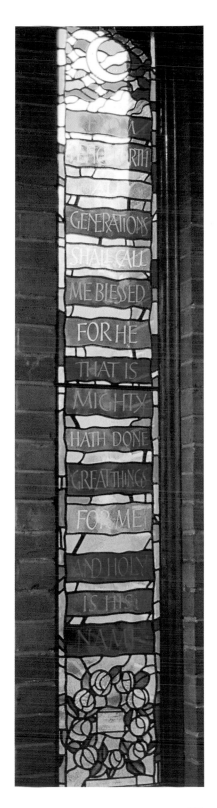

David Pilkington
The Magnificat
One of two stained glass windows, both measuring 2260 x 320mm/88.97 x 12.6in., designed by the engraver for the Lady Chapel, St Mary's Church, Rotherham. The lettering was drill engraved before the various shades of blue 'antique' glass were leaded.

CHAPTER SIXTEEN

Sending glass through the post

When sending glass to the client or recipient it should be placed within two boxes.

First box

First, wrap the item in tissue paper; then in several layers of bubble wrap (with extra round the stem of a goblet to make the padding the same diameter as that of the bowl); then place this in a box. Shake the box gently; there should be no movement from inside.

If a presentation box is used, do not wrap the glass. Instead, build up the padding beneath the fabric in the base with bubble wrap; place the cleaned glass in the box, with the correct side to view. Shake the presentation box gently; there should be no movement from inside. If there is, continue to add more padding beneath the fabric. When there is no further movement, the first box can then be wrapped in several layers of bubble wrap and placed in a second, sturdier box.

Second box

The address label, with post code, must be clearly seen. Several 'Fragile' and 'Glass with care' labels should be stuck on each side and top and base, and the address of the sender placed where it is easily seen but not so large that it can be mistaken for the addressee. Arrange appropriate insurance and, if necessary, a specialist carrier.

There can never be too much protection for the glass but it must be of the correct kind and put in the correct places; solid sheets of polystyrene do not withstand shocks sufficiently well for glass items. Polystyrene shapes or bubble wrap of various dimensions are more reliable.

CHAPTER
SEVENTEEN

Pricing work

To weigh up the time, skill and materials needed against what the market will bear has been a concern for artists and craftsmen throughout the centuries. Time is needed to develop an idea and for the actual engraving. (It is not possible to know how long a design will take to develop and this is difficult to explain to the client!) With the cost of glass, burs, perhaps a presentation box, and including the cost of postage and packaging, the total cost might be considerable.

Every artist should have some idea of a fair hourly rate. Discussions about fee should take place at the beginning of negotiations; sometimes the client will have a ceiling to which the engraver can work. It can be helpful to both parties if a quotation is presented to the client with a variable final price dependent upon agreed contingences. (Sandblasting is not necessarily 'quick'; masking up, deep blasting and cleaning off can take as long, if not longer, than drill engraving.) Occasionally it will be necessary to decline a commission; to take on work for too small a fee will devalue the artist's own work and that of others.

Having obtained a piece of engraved glass, hopefully the client will appreciate that this will be a unique possession, perhaps with personal significance, which will provide years of interest and pleasure.

Anne Irwin

Alphabet vase. 180mm/7.08in. high. The design of these sturdy, sans serif letters is influenced by the shape and weight of the vase. The letters look as though they might be monoline but, although the contrast is very slight, there is a subtle 'thick and thin' to the strokes; notice the entasis and also the slight widening at stroke endings. Using the smallest, spherical shaped diamond bur in the drill, the outlines of the letters were marked in with a fine line and then built up to provide a consistent width. In selected areas, the spaces – either outside the letter or within the counter – were also engraved to accentuate some of the many patterns formed.

Photograph by David Mocatta.

APPENDIX

Leonard Evetts (1909 – 1997)

It is a great pleasure to be able to include this profile of Leonard Evetts (1909 – 1997) which has been contributed by The Rev. Robert Cooper, presently of the Chaplaincy to the Arts and Recreation in North East England.

At the Royal College of Art, Leonard Evetts was a student of mural painting, stained glass and lettering – the last under Edward Johnston. During most of his working life he combined being Head of the Design School in the University of Newcastle with carrying out numerous commissions, often integrating glass and lettering to powerful effect. The work illustrated reveals the sureness of letter-form combined with vigorous expression to be expected of someone who had been exposed to Johnston's understanding that the essential qualities of lettering are 'Sharpness, Unity and Freedom'[1] and who was to go on to write a seminal text *Roman Lettering* (Pitman 1938, later available from A & C Black).

In later life Leonard Evetts recalled his pride at being chosen by Johnston as his demonstration student. He also looked back with delight on his teacher's ability to do quite outrageous things with lettering – 'but they were such fun and they worked'. He also never forgot the sign which read, 'For goodness sake do something careless' – careless being the closest Johnston could come to expressing what he meant. For this reason perfection remained a dead ideal for Leonard Evetts. He sought instead for life in his lettering. The appreciation of space was also a key component in his approach to design, so it is not without significance that he spoke of the alphabet as 'possibly the greatest piece of abstract art that mankind has produced'[2]. That Evetts placed as much importance on the pattern of counter-spaces as on the strokes of the letters also explains the rhythmic beauty achieved in such undemonstrative elements as the inscription

In memory of Florence Ball 1873-1969

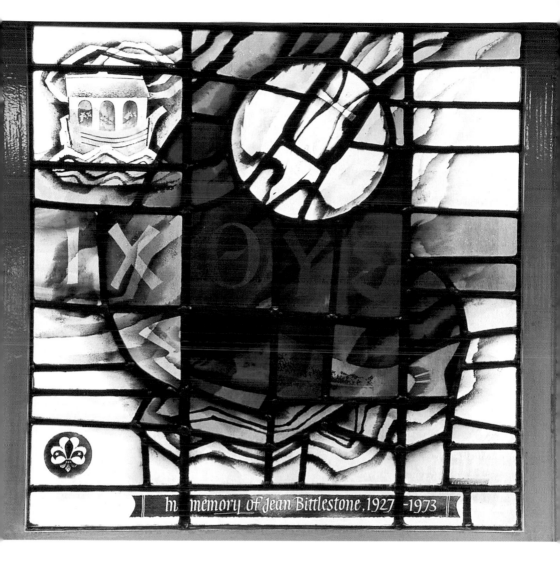

in memory of Jean Bittlestone, 1927 -1973

Left **Leonard Evetts**
St Columba of Iona window.
680 x 680mm/26.77 x 26.77in.
Reproduced by kind permission of Mrs
Phyllis Evetts and the PCC of St Nicholas'
Church, Bishopwearmouth.
Photograph by Robert Cooper.

Left below, detail

Above ΙΧΟΤΣ
Window 680 x 680mm/26.77 x 26.77in.
Reproduced by kind permission of
Mrs Phyllis Evetts and the PCC of St
Nicholas' Church, Bishopwearmouth.
Photograph by Robert Cooper.

illustrated *In memory of Florence Ball*. Note, for example, how the curve of the 'r' in 'Florence' exactly echoes the surging arch of the 'n', helping to create a marching, almost leaping, rhythm.

Christopher Wardale, one of Leonard Evetts' former students, well remembers the techniques he used in creating such lettering: 'To make an inscription such as the one *In memory of Florence Ball*, Len began by covering the glass with a thick layer of paint mixed with gum to make it fairly solid and able to retain its opacity after firing. Having tacked the glass to the window, he would cut through the paint with a quill, using a version written on paper as a guide.

Having first composed himself, he wrote these inscriptions, if possible, in one piece and at one go. If he was interrupted, he would wipe off the paint and start again. It was at this stage, or after firing, that Len would split the inscription if the leading required it'.

This description makes it clear how Leonard Evetts achieved the feat of writing on glass with the smoothness, fluency and clarity we associate with writing on parchment. Such a technique explains how he could create the classic 'one chance to get it right' feel of the versal letters in the title *St Columbus of Iona*. This is only possible when an absolute certainty of form is married with the felicitous inconsistency of the hand-made.

As Christopher Wardale recalls, Leonard Evetts took a similar approach in painting large letters such as ΙΧΟΤΣ ('fish' – the early Christian cryptogram for 'Jesus Christ, Son of God, Saviour'). 'A piece

of glass, coloured to the depth he wanted for the letter, would be washed with darker paint. After it had dried, a quill or another of the tools he made for himself, was used to remove the paint, revealing the letter. Before the firing, there might be a little scratching out or adding of paint to create texture and depth, or to create a sense of mystery. As with all his work the result appears effortless – though it was, in fact, the result of enormous skill.

'As students we were with Len in a very mediaeval way, helping him with the tasks to which our experience and ability fitted us. He was a very tough, but wonderful teacher, because he worked with you. He did not want you to be like him, but to develop skill to go beyond his work. If he saw something you had done that he liked he would ask how you did it and maybe explore the possibility himself. But, with typical generosity, he always gave you the credit!'

1 Edward Johnston, Formal Penmanship Lund Humphries, London 1971 p. 142
2 The writer gratefully acknowledges the help of Mrs Phyllis Evetts in preparing this article

CONCLUSION

Lettering and glass both suffer from the same disadvantage familiarity. Lettering in so many forms and glass for so many functions play such essential parts in our lives that they are accepted without question. Daily, our eyes are subjected to letters of good or bad shape and proportion in an assortment of sizes and of styles; we see them on buildings, on signs, and in printed material. We use items made from glass in the home and are surrounded by glass in architecture and industry. The design opportunities for combining letters with glass have yet to be fully explored.

This book has dealt mainly with two ways to engrave, with the drill and with sandblast, but with continual technological development letterers of the 21st century may discover as yet unknown ways to work with glass. Hopefully, this book will interest students of lettering and calligraphy sufficiently for them to begin a creative journey with this entrancing, beguiling, wonderful medium.

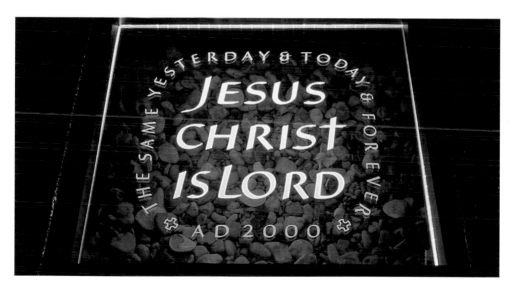

Millennium Text. At the Church of St Thomas a Becket, Pagham, Sussex, an idea by the Vicar exploits an interesting use of glass, lettering and fibre optics. Two layers of glass 100mm/3.9in. apart are set into a stainless steel box let into the floor at the west end of the aisle. The unengraved top layer of clear glass is flush with the floor. Only the engraved lower glass is lit by fibre optics. The design is handcut but sandblasted by a specialist company.

The small letters are surface engraved on the top of the lower glass and reflect on its underside (like a chorus); the large letters are deeply sandblasted on the underside but appear closer to the viewer. To emphasise contact, pebbles from a nearby beach line the box base. The words chosen are the simplest and, to complement the architecture, the design unadorned. The letters, the words, and their message, are transformed by light.

GLOSSARY

to abrade the surface to roughen the surface by pitting it with a tool

acid etch etching of design onto glass by use of acid

anneal controlled cooling of hot glass in special kiln

'antique' commercial expression for glass made to look old by the introduction of air bubbles and imitation hair line cracks

ascender stroke of minuscule (lower case) letter which begins above the writing line, eg. **h**

'back to black' clear glass again, the engraved surface is highly polished so that it looks like its unengraved state

backbone central line of a copperplate pen stroke, before nib is splayed

breathing iron blowpipe used by glass-blowing artist

bur engraving tool fitted into tip of drill; diamond or synthetic, of various shapes and sizes

collet collar on drill or pin vice that grips bur or tungsten carbide needle

composition stone man-made stone, eg. carborundum

copperplate letter a letter in copperplate style of cursive handwriting

copper wheel copper disc, fixed to a spindle inserted into a lathe (see *wheel engraving*)

crossover point where the sides of a broad pen stroke cross during letter making

cullet waste glass from glassmaking, not annealed

descender stroke of minuscule (lower case) letter which is carried below the writing line, e.g. **p**

diamond tipped scriber hand held tool for engraving glass

diamond wheel disc with industrial diamond grit, fixed to a spindle inserted into a lathe (see *wheel engraving*)

double pencils two pencils fastened together, their points level

dry method (of drill engraving) engraving without supply of water to lubricate bur

edged brush brush with flattened ferrule and straight end, not pointed

entasis the slight swelling of an outline of a column which counteracts the optical illusion of concavity that a straight column would produce: relevant to large, drawn letters

etching paste/cream form in which acid is available to engraver

flexible-drive drill based on dental drill, this has an electrical cable between engraving end and motor, controlled with a foot pedal

flourishes lines and twirls extending from letters as decoration

gather hot glass taken from kiln onto end of blowpipe

gilding application of gold

gouache water-based paint, opaque

hobby drill type of drill with motor in handpiece

hopper container (in base of small sandblast cabinet but often set apart from large industrial machines)

inlay insertion of colour or metal in engraved glass

intaglio the cutting away of areas of glass (depth can be varied)

key reference mark in ink on glass (later removed) to enable accurate positioning of design before engraving

laser beam fracturing late 20th century use of laser beams to create 2- or 3-dimensional design within glass

lathe heavy metal clamp into which a spindle may be fastened; a copper or stone or diamond wheel is then attached to the spindle for engraving

letter space amount of space between each letter; may be increased (or decreased) depending on effect desired; more often applied to capital letters than to lower case

letter weight thickness of letter stroke

in relationship to height of letter; will make letter look delicate or sturdy

line space amount of space between each line; may be altered depending on effect required

line wheel engraving wheel with profile that cuts a line (see *wheel engraving*)

mask covering or stencil applied to glass before sandblasting

micromotor type of drill with motor in handpiece

mitre wheel engraving wheel with profile that makes a V-shaped cut (see *wheel engraving*)

opaque not transparent

optical glass glass with no visible or optical impurities

pin vice can be part of scriber, designed to hold tungsten carbide needles

to polish to make the engraved surface shiny using a series of finer and finer grinding compounds

pontil/punty iron iron rod used by glassblower to carry blown glass for further decoration

pot container within a furnace for molten glass

relief engraving in the case of glass, surface round image is cut away to allow image to stand proud

sandblast (gritblast) projection of grit against glass; for short or long periods of time

sandblast cabinet cabinet in which sandblasting is carried out in order to prevent spread of grit

'scribbles' a technique of surface engraving

seed (or stone) tiny air bubble within glass, often formed accidently during the making

serif and sans serif letters with and without marks at head or foot, eg. d (with serif), **d** (sans serif).(In pen made letters, caused by the movement when beginning the stroke to make the writing medium flow and at the finish of the stroke to make a controlled stop to the flow)

sintered diamond bur (see p.39)

slumped pre-formed glass re-shaped in adjusted heat of kiln over or into a mould

slurry liquid waste

stencil a plastic mask with image (either positive or negative) for sand-blasting

stipple technique (usually with hand tool) for creating an image from separate dots

stone (see *seed*)

stone wheel engraving wheel made of man-made stone (see *wheel engraving*)

strap wheel type of engraving wheel with a profile that makes a flat cut with straight sides (like a ribbon)

stress weak point in some glass due to nature of manufacture

surface engraving where glass is stippled or abraded by a bur without areas being cut away (as in intaglio engraving)

tapered bur (rat tail) type of bur

toughened borosilicate glass type of glass which must never be used by a glass engraver (it will shatter)

tungsten carbide synthetic substance used (in glass engraving) for needles in scribers

water jet cutting late 20th century commercial engraving method that employs a powerful water jet as the tool

wet method (of drill engraving) engraving with supply of water

wheel engraving to engrave glass with a wheel (disc) fixed on a revolving spindle set into a lathe; the glass is presented to the wheel which can be made of copper or composition stone or diamond; all are available in different circumferences, profiles and thickness; (the former used with oil to lubricate and grit to make the cut, the two latter used with water to lubricate whilst making the cut); as the design is engraved, the wheels are changed to make different cuts

word space amount of space between each word in a line of lettering, only sufficient is needed to separate the groups of letters making the words

BIBLIOGRAPHY

If titles are out of print, copies might be obtained direct from second-hand bookshops or via the Internet.

The Calligrapher's Handbook Edited by Heather Child. A & C Black (Publishers) Ltd, London 1985. ISBN 0 7136 2695 X

Experimenting with Calligraphy Margaret Daubney B. T. Batsford 1995. ISBN 0 7134 76575

Calligraphy made easy Gaynor Goffe. Paragon & Robinson. ISBN 0 7525 2055 5 hardback; also hardback spiral bound and paperback

Creative Lettering Today Michael Harvey. A & C Black (Publishers) 1996. ISBN 0 7136 645768

Lessons in Formal Writing Edward Johnston. Edited by Heather Child & Justin Howes. Lund Humphries, London 1986

Formal Brush Writing Tom Kemp. Twice Publishing, Oxford; first published 1999. ISBN 0 9537 374 0 3 H; 0 9537 3741 1 P. Available from the publishers, 53 Mill Street, OX2 0AL

Historical Scripts Stan Knight. A & C Black (Publishers) Ltd, London; 1984. ISBN 0 7136 2418 3. Republished by Oak Knoll, 1998, USA

Historical Scripts: from Classical Times to the Renaissance Stan Knight. St Pauls Bibliographies, USA

The Mystic Art of Written Forms Friedrich Neugebauer Verlag Neugebauer Press, Salzburg 1979. Translated by Bruce Kennett, English text 1980 Neugebauer Press Publishing Ltd. ISBN 0 907234 00

Tom Perkins Lettercarver. Published 1998 by Calligraphic Enterprises, Ditchling, Sussex

A Book of Formal Scripts John Woodcock, historical notes by Stan Knight. A & C Black (Publishers) Ltd, London; first published 1992. ISBN 0 7136 3245 3

The Techniques of Glass Engraving Jonathan Matcham & Peter Dreiser. B T Batsford, London; first published 1982. ISBN 0 7134 2536 9

Glass Engraving: Drill Techniques Stuart & Shirley Palmer. B T Batsford, London; 1990

Glass Engraving: Lettering & Design David Peace. B T Batsford, London; first published 1985. ISBN 0 7134 3954 8

The History of Glass Edited by Dan Klein & Ward Lloyd. Orbis Publishing Ltd 1984, reprinted Macdonald & Co (Publishers) Ltd. 1989. ISBN 0 7481 0246 9

Glass Edited by Reino Liefkes. V&A Publications, London; first published 1997. ISBN 1851771980

Five Thousand Years of Glass Edited by Hugh Tait. British Museum Press, London; first published 1991. ISBN 0 7141 1716 1

Societies

Current addresses for the following societies can be found in the telephone directory or on the internet. Many welcome non-practising members. The last two listed are concerned with the history of glass and collections.

Calligraphy & Lettering Arts Society
Society of Scribes & Illuminators
The Guild of Glass Engravers
Contemporary Glass Society
The Scottish Glass Society
The Glass Association
The Glass Circle

INDEX